When Love Was Like That
and Other Stories

Marie Joseph was born in Lancashire and was educated at Blackburn High School for Girls. Before her marriage she was in the Civil Service. She now lives in Middlesex with her husband, a retired chartered Engineer, and they have two married daughters and eight grandchildren.

Marie Joseph began her writing career as a short-story writer and she now uses her Northern background to enrich her bestselling novels. Down-to-earth characters bring a vivid authenticity to her stories, which are written with both humour and poignancy.

Her novel **A BETTER WORLD THAN THIS** won the 1987 Romantic Novelist's Association Major Award.

WHEN LOVE
WAS LIKE THAT
and Other Stories

Marie Joseph

ARROW

Arrow Books Limited
20 Vauxhall Bridge Road, London SW1V 2SA

An imprint of Random House UK Ltd

London Melbourne Sydney Auckland Johannesburg
and agencies throughout the world

First published in 1991 by Century
Arrow edition 1992

3 5 7 9 10 8 6 4

Printed and bound in Great Britain by
Cox & Wyman Ltd, Reading, Berkshire

ISBN 0 09 997060 0

05615043

Contents

Time Will Tell   1
Little Dreamer   9
I Love Paris in the Springtime   19
Have Typewriter – Will Travel   29
The Perfect Wife   39
Are You Listening Miranda?   47
Mr Fix-it   53
The Gentle Man   61
Please, Please Noel   75
If Only We Could Lock Up Linda   85
Different from the Rest   89
Plain Jane   99
To Remember for Always   107
Dominic   113
Visiting Time   119
Dream of Tomorrow   123
Unknown Admirer   127
The Comforters   131
Fancy Seeing You Here   135
What Kind of Girl Am I?   141
The Drama   149
The Christening   155
To Love and Let Go   159
Love is Like That   165
Skip the Fish Course for Me   177
Hello You   185
The Up-Thinker   191
The Power of Love   199
No More Mountains   209
Conversation for One   223
The Last Link   229

Time Will Tell

Slowly, so as not to wake him, Louise eased her body away from Adam, her husband, and got out of bed. She had been awake for a long time, watching the changing swiftness of an Italian April dawn light the sky, hearing the muted sounds of the hotel coming to life, hearing the first swish of tyres as cars drove past along the coast road.

There were rose-pearled clouds banked high on the horizon, and the sea, a smooth spread of silk, reflected the pale washed-out colour of a sky not yet deepened to blue by the sun.

'The uncertain glory of an April day,' she thought, and smiled. Not at heart a girl who often quoted poetry, she felt that a woman, any woman on the second morning of her honeymoon, could be excused for becoming just a little lyrical . . .

For a moment she breathed deeply of the air which she could only describe to herself as smelling 'foreign', and she remembered Adam's incredulous disbelief when she had told him that she had never been abroad.

In the two months since they met at a Valentine party, given on a damp February evening, he had never stopped being amazed at what he called her unworldliness.

'Girls like you don't exist any more,' he had told her. 'Not in nineteen-seventy-one . . . Nineteen years old, still living at home with Mama, virginal,' he had said, with that humorous lift of one black eyebrow. 'Girls like you went out with Jane Austen, and suitors proposing on bended knee.'

But he had proposed to her, just three weeks after they'd met.

Was it because she baffled him so much that he'd asked her to marry him, instead of suggesting that she merely moved into his flat? Was that why he'd behaved like the old-fashioned suitor he certainly wasn't, restricting his love-making to kisses which left her weak and trembling, and wanting him with a longing at complete and utter variance with his preconceived image of her?

Turning away now from the open balcony window, she stared at him with grave intensity.

Nine years older than she, he slept with the abandon of a very young boy, his black hair tousled, an overnight stubble on his chin, aggressively male, an unconscious stranger.

Shivering a little in her shortie nightdress, she closed the window, taking care not to make any sound; padding softly on bare feet back to the bed, she sat down, and with wifely possessiveness, watched him sleep.

So this was it. This was what being married meant – this rather empty, flat feeling that . . . surely this wasn't all there was to it? Was this to be the pattern of her life from now on? Were all the books she'd read, all the films she'd seen with their emphasis on the bedroom scenes, all the sly, teasing remarks of the girls at the office, just one big build-up to an experience which for her had been nothing more than a disappointing let-down?

Of course she had wondered how it would be; of course she had imagined lying in his arms, giving herself to him utterly, filled with such ecstasy that she could scarcely breathe.

'Honeymoons are hell.' She'd read that too, and smiled at the assumption. She remembered smiling and thinking that that couldn't possibly apply to her and Adam. Not when they loved each other so much – not when they'd *waited*. Not after he'd suffered what she knew he'd looked upon as the indignity of a conventional church wedding, with her mother sitting in the front pew, eyes suitably dewy, and Lance, Adam's friend from university days, winking at her with wicked amusement as she came down the aisle in her white midi-dress, her long brown hair threaded with flowers.

'What has old Adam let himself in for?' his expression said, and in the plane, after a brief reception in the local roadhouse, she had sensed Adam's relief.

'Well, I played it your way,' he seemed to be saying, 'and now I can show you what love, really loving a man, can mean.'

She wasn't the first. He'd been quite honest about that, and she didn't mind, not if she didn't think about it too much. It was better that a husband should be experienced; she'd read that too. But it had been over before she'd realised it had begun. Certainly there had been a genuine passion on Adam's side, but on hers — nothing.

She sighed deeply, and turned to look out of the window again. He'd slept immediately, as if she didn't exist, as if there were nothing more, no gentle words, no companionship, and in the morning they'd overslept.

Yesterday they had walked miles along the coast road, lunching on wine and cheese, and coming back to the hotel to dine by candlelight, and she was sure this time it would be different.

Different, only in that she had been even lonelier when the moonlight glided in at the window, finding her sleepless and dismayed. In the early hours she fell asleep, a heavy sleep, from which she woke to this pale dawn.

'Louise?' Adam's voice was thick with sleep. 'What are you doing out of bed? What time is it?'

She told him, and he stretched out a hand and gripped her arm.

3

'You're cold, love. Come here, come and get warm.'

'No, I'll go and get dressed,' she said, and tried to pull away, but his grip on her arm tightened.

She met his eyes, she had to, she couldn't do anything else, not when he was holding her like that, and now it was his turn to look away. Raising himself on one elbow, he reached across the bed for his cigarettes on the table.

'Want one?' he offered, and she shook her head.

This wasn't the way all the books she had read, all the films she had seen, had made her believe it would be . . .

In them the bride woke up, turned her head and saw her husband lying beside her, stretched her arms high above her head, completely and utterly fulfilled. Drugged with a surfeit of love, recalling on the instant she awoke the pleasure, the shared delight, the precious moments when romance became love.

Curling her toes on the carpet, Louise examined the pink polish so lovingly applied, just one small item of grooming in her excited preparation for what was to be.

All the preparations so lovingly undertaken . . . The pale blue lace and the white, the matching negligees, the perfume selected after so much discussion with the girl on the cosmetic counter -- and for what? For this lonely vigil in the dawn, for moments so short that all they gave her was a sense of her own inadequacy . . .

What was the use, really? All the bridal decorations . . . did they only serve to mask the emptiness that women found in marriage? Or (and this troubled her deeply) was she to blame? Other women, perhaps, found happiness; for them the orange blossom, the champagne, the pretty trimmings – these were a true expression of an inner happiness which came to them on the honeymoon. She found only disappointment.

Adam was watching her. 'What are you thinking about, love?'

'Nothing,' she said quickly.

Stubbing out the half-smoked cigarette, he moved over to make room for her, lifting up the satin-bound blanket. 'Come on,' he ordered, and with what she had to admit, even to herself, was a martyred sigh, she reluctantly did as she was told.

But to her surprise, he made no attempt to take her in his arms. Instead, they lay side by side in the frilled bed, like strangers. She qualified that: not like strangers, but like a married couple, used to each other, *bored* with each other, only disillusionment ahead.

'It's going to be another fine day,' he said politely, and equally politely she agreed that he could be right.

And all unbidden, a snippet of conversation she remembered from years before, came into her mind. It was just after her mother's divorce, and with a friend she was discussing the idiosyncrasies, the vagaries, the shortcomings of men.

Heedless of the thirteen-year-old girl placidly getting on with her homework in the corner, her mother had elaborated, mouthing the words she was sure her daughter was too young to comprehend.

'Thank God that part of it's over, and I don't need to *pretend* any more. Don't you think most women pretend?'

The friend had agreed; Louise had got on with her drawing of a map of the Industrial Midlands, and forgotten the conversation.

. . . Until now, as she lay by her husband's side, two whole days married, and a whole life of pretending ahead.

Adam's voice came muffled from the adjoining pillow. 'I'm sorry, love,' he said.

'Sorry for what?' she asked, still deep in her own thoughts.

'For failing you,' he said.

Some feminine instinct made her lie still, making no attempt to turn to him. 'Failing me?' she said.

'It wasn't much good, was it?' he said, and she nearly said, 'Don't be silly,' but now she knew the time for pretending was over, and lay quietly by his side, waiting for him to go on.

'I meant it to be so different, but that first time, the beauty of you, the softness of your skin . . . I lost control. I frightened you.'

She held her breath. 'Just a little,' she admitted.

He raised himself on one elbow, and leaned over, and to her astonishment, she saw what surely couldn't be a tear, glistening in the corner of his eye.

'And last night. It was no good either. You put me off.'

'Put you off!'

'You were trying so hard to pretend you enjoyed making love . . .'

'I don't like talking about it,' she said. 'It seems awful just talking about it like this, and if you must know, I'm sorry, too.'

'For what, Louise?'

'Not coming up to expectation.'

Gently he touched her hair, lifting a strand, and twining it round his finger.

'We've got to talk about it, don't you see? It's something that married people have to talk about. It's important to be able to talk about it, especially right at the beginning. It can be the most wonderful thing if they trust each other and love each other. The most wonderful and marvellous thing.'

And because she was embarrassed and shy, she said the first thing that came to her mind. 'It's not fair!'

6

'What isn't?'

'That you should know so much about it . . . I wasn't the first.'

'But with you . . . oh Louise, my love, my little love, I meant it to be so different. I'm sorry.'

For a long moment of time they didn't speak, while outside the closed door of the honeymoon suite, the hotel came to life. There were quick footsteps in the corridor outside, the slam of a door, the sound of increased traffic in the road below.

She was only nineteen, and right from the beginning he had been amazed at her unworldliness. He was the only man she had ever given herself to, ever wanted, and she knew that what she said now was important, so important that it could affect their whole future.

For a man to admit his . . . she groped in her mind for a word . . . his inadequacy was a brave thing to do, an incredibly *manly* thing to do, and she hadn't been mistaken, it had been a tear glistening in the corner of his eye.

At the thought of that, tenderness flooded her, and a love so great that it seemed her very bones would liquefy with it. In that moment she was all compassion, and in spite of her youthfulness, all woman.

Turning towards him, she put her arms round him, holding him tight, until she felt him relax against her. Without speaking a word she stroked his hair, every touch of her fingers conveying the love she felt for him. Slowly and infinitely gently she stroked his hair, feeling the springy thickness of it, down to where it grew long in the nape of his neck; conveying by touch, all her love for him.

Then, with a sigh that was almost a groan, he kissed her, and it was all she had dreamed it would be.

This was what it was all about, was her last coherent thought before her senses swam . . .

And afterwards, they lay together in the languor of love, of blissful, married love; and then they got up and showered together, giggling and splashing like children, heedless of the fact that they would be very late for breakfast, not caring a jot one way or the other for the sly looks they knew would be levelled in their direction.

When they were dressed they went out on to the balcony, and now the sun was up, the sky had changed to a deep azure blue.

Arms around each other they stared out over the sea, and she smiled softly to herself, and thought how wrong Shakespeare had been when he had written about the uncertain glory of an April day.

It was there, spread before them in all its beauty . . .

The glory, the *certain* glory of that April day.

Little Dreamer

My daughter's name is Della. She is seven years old, much too thin, and far too serious, and will not be told that a fact is a fact, even by a kind-hearted father like me.

She still believes in Father Christmas, and she stared at me with pity when I tried to explain to her where babies really come from, so I gave up. I teased her about her freckles, and she told me in all seriousness that she had seen a sun fairy swoop down from the sky and had actually felt a gentle plonk as it deposited a few on her snub nose . . .

She attends a primary school where they firmly channel their pupils into streams, A, B and C, and her teacher this year is Miss Brown. A Miss Jenny Brown.

One day she sent me a letter:

'*Dear Mr Barton, I would very much like to have a talk with you about Della. If you cannot manage a day-time appointment, perhaps you will let me know, and we can arrange for me to call round one evening. I am, yours very sincerely, Jenny Brown.*'

I held the letter in my hand and thought for a while about Miss Brown . . . Early forties, I decided, tweed skirts, twin set, greying hair in a too-tight perm, and quarter-to-three feet in sensible shoes . . . Dedicated to her job, and worried about Della, who will not be told even by a teacher that a fact is a fact.

I found my daughter in the garden, sitting in a wigwam she had concocted from a clothes-horse and an old grey moth-eaten blanket.

'What did you do at school today?' I asked, then added hastily: 'I come, of course, to smoke the pipe of peace.'

9

Della sighed at me, and her broad forehead wrinkled itself into little tram-lines of anxiety.

'Sums, Daddy, and World Affairs.'

Now I knew the reason for the letter. Della can be quite illuminating about World Affairs.

'We had to write about the moon,' she was saying, and the nose with the plonked-on freckles wrinkled in disgust. 'I only said that it was made of soft cheese, and that big giants live there, and that when they walk, they leave their footprints in the cheese. Miss Brown showed us photographs and I could see the footprints as plain as anything. I saw them,' she added defiantly, 'as plain as plain.'

I tried to look stern.

'Della, love. You remember, we watched the television coverage of men going to the moon. You heard the three astronauts describe what they actually saw. The moon is uninhabited, there are no giants' footprints, you know that very well. And I'm sure Miss Brown explained about the craters too.'

Della's chin set itself into familiar stubbornness, and I knew that I was wasting my time. So I crawled in a most undignified fashion from the little tent with my bowler and briefcase, and went indoors to compose a note to Miss Jenny Brown. I would cancel my last two afternoon appointments, I decided, and arrange to see her the very next day.

I would go to the school and I would agree with her that in this year of nineteen-sixty-nine, when a child of seven would not believe facts that three brave men risked their lives to prove, then it's time for something to be done . . .

I parked my car in the school yard, and Miss Bywaters, the headmistress, came out of her room, and told me that she herself would supervise First Year Juniors, Stream A, while I had my chat with Miss Brown. I could see by the way her keen eyes pitied me that she, too, was worried at Della's inability to face facts that have been proven beyond any possibility of doubt.

I was studying a frieze on the wall depicting the four seasons when Miss Brown came into the room, and I held out my hand and hoped that the surprise did not show on my face.

For Miss Jenny Brown had long, pale gold hair, tied back with a black velvet ribbon. Her dress was the same clear yellow as the chrysanthemums on Miss Bywater's desk, and her skirt was a good three inches above her very pretty knees.

We came straight to the point, very business-like.

'Della has an extremely vivid imagination,' said Miss Brown. On this fact we were in immediate agreement. 'But she is old enough now to accept that a fact is a fact.'

'Especially when it comes to World Affairs,' I said, and Miss Brown glanced at me quickly to see if I was laughing, but I was perfectly serious, so she carried on.

By the way, she had two little dimples at the corners of her mouth, which appeared and disappeared as she talked, and I was finding this most distracting . . .

'Forgive me for mentioning this, Mr Barton, but how long is it since your wife died?'

'Almost five years, Miss Brown.'

'And you have brought Della up entirely alone?'

I told her about the maiden aunt who stayed for two years, then went to live with her sister in Cumberland, and the succession of daily helps, and the glamorous au-pair girl who caused so much speculation amongst the neighbours before she went back to Sweden to marry her fiancé, and I told her about the kind neighbour across the road with four children of her own, who looked after Della until I came home from work and during school holidays and half-term.

Miss Brown nodded, and walked over to the window so that a sudden shaft of sunlight turned her hair to spun gold.

'The other day I got the children to write a composition about one of their parents,' she told me, 'and Della wrote about her mother. She wrote about her as though she were still alive. Your daughter has a flair for words, Mr Barton. She described how, when she is in bed at night, her mother, who is small and dark and rather plump, comes into her room smelling of apple-scented talcum powder, and tucks her in with gentle fingers . . .' She paused, and her voice was all kindness. 'Would she remember her mother as clearly as that, do you think?'

I shook my head, and decided not to tell her that Della's mother was tall and red-haired, and definitely not the tucking-in type.

'Della doesn't remember her mother at all,' I said, and Miss Brown turned round to face me, her blue eyes troubled.

'You see?' she said.

I said that indeed I did. Then I asked her what, if anything, was to be done?

'She must not be encouraged to daydream so much. And perhaps if you were to be firm with her every time she indulges in these flights of fancy? Some day she is going to be hurt very much if she is allowed to make up her own stories about the way things are. Life is too real for that,' said Miss Brown, and I had to agree.

'I want to help her to see things the way they are,' she said, and held out her hand, and I promised to co-operate.

Outside in the cold, grey, asphalt playground, the sun had gone in, and the loneliness I had refused to admit to for a long time, enveloped me like the thick blanket of Della's wigwam.

For the next few days I thought a lot about our problems, and it gave me a warm sort of feeling to know that someone was worrying along with me. I watched

Della carefully and she seemed normal enough to me.

She played with her dolls, and tried to persuade me for the umpteenth time to buy her a kitten, and for the umpteenth time I explained that with no one in the house all day, to have a kitten would not only be impossible but downright unkind.

'It is out of the question, Della, love,' I said, remembering my promise to Miss Brown.

My daughter's eyes have dreams shimmering in their depths, and she stared at me, but said nothing.

When I called her in for her bath, she was out in the garden talking to someone. 'Who was that?' I asked, and her eyes met mine unflinchingly.

'Snowball, my kitten, she said, and as I ran the water, she undressed and stood there on the bath-mat in her birthday-suit, so thin and beautiful that my heart ached with the real pain of love.

'I called him Snowball because he is white. All over,' she said. 'And his eyes are green, and he likes it best of all when I roll him over on his back and tickle his tummy. He likes that best of all.'

For a moment I forgot Miss Brown and the problem we shared.

'Is he with us now, in the bathroom?' I asked, and Della flashed me a look of scorn.

'He hates the water, Daddy, and he won't come inside, because he can hear the taps running, and he thinks we may be going to bath him.'

Climbing into the tub, she gave a little shudder because I hadn't added quite enough hot water.

'He's outside on the landing, waiting for me.'

I soaped her straight little back and realised that I was encouraging her flight of fancy. My conscience pricked me as I remembered Miss Brown's anxious eyes, and I pulled myself together. I must keep my side of the bargain if we were to bring Della out of her dream world.

So gently but firmly I said: 'Della, love, you have no little kitten. You know we can't have a kitten, and you can't carry on a conversation with someone who isn't there. It's rather silly, you know.' It had absolutely no effect.

My daughter made a fist and squeezed the soap so that the bubbles came through. 'He's crying outside the door. I mustn't stay in the bath too long. He gets very nervous when I'm not there.'

That evening I couldn't settle to anything. Not to my books or the television, or the lawn crying out to be mowed. The loneliness I thought I'd conquered threatened to swamp me again.

I stared at the telephone and decided that my problem was too big for one person to shoulder alone. But I was dismayed to find, that even in our small local directory, there are four whole pages of Browns, so feeling like a traitor, I went upstairs and found Della was still awake, because as she explained, Snowball insisted on sleeping on her bed, and woke up and mewed every time she moved her feet.

He was reasonably good while she told me that Miss Brown lived in one of the flats by the bridge, on the top-most floor, so high that when she went out on her balcony she could touch the stars.

'Did Miss Brown tell you that?' I asked, and Della's clear blue glance of scorn sent me back downstairs to leaf through the telephone directory with renewed determination.

Miss Brown listened to me, and she agreed that there seemed to be plenty to discuss, and promised to have dinner with me the very next day.

She wore a black dress with a halter neck-line and a big chunk cut away at the back, and her hair on top of her head attractively arranged in bright gold coils.

We ate at the Crown, at a table in a secluded alcove,

and we talked for a long time before we got around to discussing little Della and the problem we shared.

I asked her a lot of questions and she didn't seem to mind. She told me that her parents lived in the north of England, that she was twenty-five, and that once she was engaged to be married, but it was broken off, and now she lived alone, and was quite happy, thank you very much.

I began to see why she thought that life was so earnest, and why she was determined that Della must see that too, and I told her about Snowball, and she smiled at me.

'If it was just the one thing, it wouldn't matter. I used to pretend that I had a little dog called Nell,' she told me. I could see her with two fair plaits, running through the long grass with an imaginary dog hurling itself after her, but I didn't tell her that just then.

Oh, no, we talked seriously about my daughter, and I ran her home, and she made coffee and we took it out on the little balcony, because it was a lovely evening, warm and soft, with the sky jammed full of stars, and Della was right – they seemed so near that you had only to reach up your hand and touch them.

Miss Brown said that arithmetic seemed to be Della's stumbling block at the moment, on account of the fact that she will not believe that two and two make four, and although Miss Bywaters was definitely against the idea of outside coaching, she saw no reason why perhaps a few extra sums at the weekends should do her any lasting harm . . .

For this reason I invited her for tea the following Sunday, and she said that she would make a sponge cake as she was sure that I never ate any but the frozen shop kind, and I had to confess that she was right.

'And very often I forget to de-frost it in time,' I confessed, and Miss Brown laughed. The sound of her laughter stayed with me all the way down in the lift, and I found that I was counting the days until Sunday.

She arrived promptly at four o'clock and she was wearing a blue dress which exactly matched the amazing hyacinth blue of her eyes. Then I told her so, surprising myself, and she blushed.

Then, after she had handed over a cake-tin, she asked for Della, and I pointed through the window to the blanket wigwam.

'In there, probably conjuring up more fairy stories, and Snowball is there by the apple tree, sunning himself and purring.'

Miss Brown didn't laugh.

'On Friday morning, during break, I overheard Della telling two of her friends that she has recently acquired a baby brother. Called Jason, and coal black all over.'

I laughed until tears came to my eyes, but Miss Brown didn't see the joke. Her face was serious and intent, and the blue, blue eyes were clouded with anxiety.

'For a child to lie like that is a sign of severe insecurity, Mr Barton. I hope you will forgive me for mentioning this, but have you ever thought of marrying again?'

I couldn't speak, because the truth hit me like a hammer. How could I tell her that the thought had been with me since the precise moment that she walked into Miss Bywater's office, with the sunlight glinting in her wonderful golden hair?

I was mercifully prevented from answering, as Della ran into the kitchen, holding the door open carefully for Snowball to follow, and when she saw Miss Brown her little pointed face went all pink with excitement and she talked too quickly, a sure sign that she was happy and shy.

'Would you like to see my kitten, Miss Brown?' she asked. 'He is all white, until he rolls over and shows his tummy, which is a sort of pink.'

*

16

I held my breath, issues too complex to comprehend racing round in my brain. If Miss Brown rejected Snowball, if she told Della the truth, I knew that the dream I had dreamed since I first met her would be trampled into the tiled floor we stood upon.

I found myself saying a small, silent, hopeful prayer.

Then Miss Brown knelt down, and gently stroked the empty air. 'What a little darling,' she said, and her lovely face was soft with love, the way a woman's face is when she touches a kitten. Or a baby.

Della jumped up and down with joy, and for the rest of the day she didn't mention Snowball at all. We played Pig in the Middle in the garden with her big red ball, and we ate our tea round the kitchen table, ignoring the little tables I had set out all ready in the drawing-room.

We laughed a lot, and when Della had gone at last to bed, protesting on every step, we sat and talked, Miss Brown and I, watching the shadows outside change from lilac to purple, from purple to black.

We walked in the garden and by the apple tree I took her in my arms and kissed her, and I told her that between us I thought we would be able to solve our problem about Della in a most satisfactory way.

And snuggling her head on to my shoulder, Miss Brown agreed.

Then I showed her the moon, riding high in all its silvery splendour, and she watched it for a while, then laughed out loud.

'They're very plain to see tonight,' she said, and still bemused by the nearness of her, I asked her what on earth she meant.

'Why, the giant's footprints, of course,' said Miss Brown. 'If you look carefully, there they are. As plain as plain can be . . .'

17

I Love Paris in the Springtime

It is said that if you stand at Piccadilly Circus for long enough, someone you know will eventually pass by, so I see no reason why the same theory shouldn't apply to the Eiffel Tower.

Anyway, Madame had assembled the girls into some sort of ragged order, and I was bringing up the rear – and thinking about all the songs that had been written about Paris in the spring, and wondering how the lyric writers would have gone on if they'd had twenty giggling girls to contend with – when I saw him.

He, in his turn, was encumbered with a good round dozen or so of English schoolboys, who had apparently just gone totally berserk at the unexpected sight of a bunch of their female compatriots.

'Come along, Bateson,' he was saying. 'How can I book *en bloc*, if you will insist on diverging?'

And as Bateson cast a last, burning glance at Sandra Stubbs, the glamour girl of my little lot, he was manhandled roughly into line.

It was the voice that did it. After all, most Englishmen in hacking jackets with their dark brown hair needing a trim, look pretty much the same.

Guy Gerrard, I thought. Well, well. And as we formed our charges into an acceptable crocodile, and marched them down some avenue or other, I was back four years, to my last night at college, dancing with Guy Gerrard at the end-of-term dance, and being made passionately innocent love to at four o'clock in the morning, before being pushed through my hostel window.

He'd sworn, if not undying love, at least the promise

19

of forthcoming devotion, and as we were comparative strangers, he'd written down my home address and telephone number on the back of a dry-cleaner's ticket. He'd said that after he came back from Greece – or it could have been Yugoslavia – we must meet and carry on from where we were pleasantly leaving off.

And that had been that.

Neither hair nor hide of him had I seen since then, as my Yorkshire grandmother would have said, and after a while, I'd shrugged him off as one of the ships that pass in the night.

At twenty, with all the world my beckoning oyster, ships came and went, leaving barely a ripple in their wake, and living on my own soon afterwards for the first time in my life, and teaching at a large comprehensive school in North London, I soon forgot Guy Gerrard and his promises that came to nothing.

Barbie Martindale, the 'Troubleshooter' as she was nicknamed in the Staff Room, stopped with disconcerting suddenness, to extract a mythical stone from her shoe, and I almost fell full length over her.

'Did you see those drippy boys, Miss Aston?' she asked me, and as boys of any size, shape or nationality, are the sole topic of conversation amongst my form, I said, 'Which boys, Barbie?'

She flashed me a look of withering scorn. 'Why, those English boys, Miss, going up the Eiffel Tower, when we were coming out.'

'*La Tour Eiffel*, Barbie,' I said. 'Try to speak French, dear. You know the rules.'

She exchanged a pitying glance with her best friend, and I heard them say something about Old Crabby Aston. In the mood I was in, I'd have asked her to repeat that in French – if I'd known the French word for crabby.

After walking for what seemed like miles, or rather

kilometres, Madame arranged us all at little tables at a pavement café, and all the girls ordered an orange drink.

So we sat there, Madame and I at our little table, with the white-aproned *garçons* doing miraculous feats of acrobatics with their small round trays, and the sun shining down on us, a Parisian sun from a cloudless sky.

A couple of French boys strolled past, and stopped at the table where Sandra Stubbs sat, her long blonde hair falling in what she thought of as a sexy wave over one eye.

'I take your photo, yes?' they said.

And Madame, who had eyes in the back of her head, said sharply '*Non!*'

Barbie said that, compared to English boys, French boys were really something, so her excitement when the home-spun lot we'd seen at the Eiffel Tower came into view, was a study in hypocrisy . . .

This time Guy Gerrard saw me, pondered for a long unflattering moment, recognised me, and came straight to our table. 'Well!' he said, and I knew that he'd forgotten my name. 'If it isn't . . .'

'Judi Aston,' I finished for him, knowing that if Madame suspected he was any kind of pick-up, she'd have moved him on without a single French qualm.

He grinned, and oh, his grin was the most welcome sight I'd seen in the whole two weeks of tramping the streets of Paris, in company that was overwhelmingly feminine.

'May I?' he said, and with a tact I wouldn't have credited Madame with, she stood up, massive in the inevitable black, and moved to a nearby table to chaperone our little party, who were now giggling themselves paralytic.

Leaning back in his chair, Guy smiled at me with gratifying delight.

21

'Fancy seeing you here,' we both said together, and he told me that in his rôle of teacher of European History at a school in the East End of London, he had been press-ganged into bringing the Lower Fifth to Paris for a part of their Easter vacation.

'Never again,' he said, taking a large white handkerchief from his pocket, and mopping his forehead with it. 'Whoever coined the phrase "Innocents Abroad" was singularly misinformed. Only last night I missed one of my tribe, and found him with a pocket-sized Brigitte Bardot in a doorway in Montmartre. He had the effrontery to tell me that he was studying the style *au Simenon*, and was assimilating copy for a short story he intends to write.'

'Bateson?' I asked him, and his eyebrows raised themselves clean over his glass of beer.

'I saw you at the Eiffel Tower,' I explained. 'I had just finished mopping up a nose-bleed, brought on by the great height, so I was informed by the hypochondriac of our little lot.'

'Were we like that at thirteen and fourteen?' he asked. I shook my head.

'I never was thirteen,' I told him sadly. 'Springtime in Paris hasn't managed to raise my blood-pressure by as much as a single notch up to now.'

'Had them up the steps of the *Notre Dame*?' he asked me grimly. I nodded.

'Three hundred and ninety-eight steps, I was told. The hypo was sick all over the three hundred and fourth.'

He laughed out loud, and as Madame busily gathered our brood together, he spoke quickly. 'Any evenings off?'

Reluctantly I stood up. 'We've only one day left.'

Madame stared rather pointedly in my direction.

'What's on the itinerary tomorrow?' he said, and I

told him a conducted tour of *La Concièrgerie* in the morning, and a margarine factory in the afternoon.

'Come along, girls. *No* loitering,' said Madame, and Guy Gerrard winked at me, and said something I didn't catch.

And we didn't have to wait until the morrow before we met again. Three times our paths crossed – by the flower-sellers outside the *Madeleine*, on the *Métro* platform, and in the camera shop, where *we* were collecting our newly developed films, and *he* was talking cameras to a lovely French girl.

Eventually Madame and I got the girls safely back to the rather forbidding *château* where we were domiciled, the longest delay resulting from losing Barbie and Sandra as we came out of the *Métro* station. Or maybe their explanation that they had lost *us* was nearer the truth. By that time I wouldn't have cared if we'd never seen either of them again.

Seeing Guy Gerrard talking to the French girl like that had reminded me forcibly of the days I'd spent after our short-lived affair, mooning round the house, willing the telephone to ring. Pointless days, staring down the avenue, looking for the postman, never quite believing that he wasn't going to write. Looking in vain for a postcard from Greece, or was it Yugoslavia?

Long after I'd started my first job, and moved into a flat of my own, I would ask my mother was she sure that a letter hadn't arrived for me. Then the gradual acceptance of the fact that I had been merely a girl to while away the last evening of his sojourn at university took root, and I forced myself to forget him.

At least, I had thought that I had forgotten him . . .

In all probability, I had told myself, he had a fiancée somewhere, who had spent the past three years being faithful to him. In all probability he was married to her now. But no, he hadn't had a married look about him at all, I decided, and the decision was strangely comforting.

'Miss?' Barbie asked me that same evening over steak and salad. 'Was that dishy man your boyfriend, Miss?'

Her best friend giggled obligingly, and putting her head on one side, Barbie said, 'What is the French for *lover*, Miss?'

The girls spent the evening washing and setting each other's hair on jumbo rollers, and listening to pop records that had accompanied them across the Channel. At ten-thirty I was more than relieved to see them all into their respective beds in the big dormitory, and to crawl into mine in the room next door.

At half-past eleven I heard a noise, and caught Barbie and retinue creeping Indian-file along the corridor, giggling themselves silly after a raid on the pantry. Each and every one of them clutched a block of chocolate, and they left a trail of pineapple juice behind them, like a liquid paper-chase.

After I'd treated them to a shortened version of the riot act, they told me pathetically that girls at boarding-schools always had midnight feasts, and they were only living the part, as it were, and who would miss a few bars of chocolate and a few measly bottles of pineapple juice, anyway, and now it was all spoiled because some people couldn't be sporty about anything.

I went back to bed feeling vaguely ashamed of myself, and the worst sport of all time, to boot.

The following morning Madame hired an autobus, and we drove off in great style.

La Conciergerie had the girls spellbound, and they drank in every morbid detail about the prisoners once kept there. The tiny cell which had housed Marie Antoinette for six tortuous weeks filled them with delighted awe.

We were shown the knife of the guillotine, and the

hypochondriac came over faint when Barbie bemoaned the lack of blood stains, and had to be taken out to recover.

'Was it really true, Miss,' Sandra Stubbs asked me, 'that Marie Antoinette was watched over night and day by twelve guards, Miss?'

I assured her that this was perfectly true, and there was a concerted nudging and giggling. 'You mean that they didn't leave her for *one* minute, Miss?'

We were being shown round a tiny courtyard with high walls with iron bars atop, where the prisoners were reputed to have taken the air, when Guy Gerrard and his boys arrived.

Immediately poor Marie Antoinette and her embarrassing privations were forgotten, and the two sides greeted each other with rapturous joy.

Disapproval emanated from Madame, and the tumbrils couldn't have been filled with greater speed and determination than was our waiting autobus.

We drove away with someone saying something about frustrated spinsters in particular, and bad old sports in general. I sat on the front seat, with Madame spilling over on to my half, and tried to remember exactly what it was that Guy had whispered to me.

'On the steps of the *Sacré-Coeur* tonight at ten o'clock. I'll wait for an hour.'

The jibe about frustrated spinsters had stung, and I turned to Madame. 'I would like to go out this evening, Madame, if that can be arranged?'

She gave me the French equivalent of an old-fashioned look. 'Very well, Mademoiselle. I will sit with the girls. It is after all, your last night in Paris.'

'Thank you, Madame,' I said.

'Not at all,' Madame told me graciously.

The margarine factory was a bit of a let-down after the *Concièrgerie*, and the girls accepted their free gifts of cookery books with scant enthusiasm.

'Well, at least,' I told myself, 'I *am* going out tonight. Tonight I will walk hand in hand with Guy Gerrard underneath a starry Parisian sky; tonight I will realise for the first time what all those writers were getting at when they went on about spring in Paris, and chestnuts in blossom.'

I worked myself up into quite a romantic lather about our meeting and, spraying myself lavishly with the French perfume I had bought to take home as a present for my mother, I left Madame presiding over twenty foot-sore and weary girls, and set off for my assignation.

Guy Gerrard had whispered that he would wait for an hour, but the way it turned out, it was I who did the waiting. A dubious French type with a scruffy little beard was trying in vain to pick me up, when Guy panted up to me.

'Bateson's gone missing again,' he said. 'We missed him at the nine o'clock count-down, and one of the boys told me that he thought he'd heard him making a date with one of your little lot in the *Concièrgerie* this morning.'

'But there wasn't time,' I protested, and Guy Gerrard's blue eyes twinkled at me. '*We* managed it,' he said, 'and anyway, you don't know Bateson. Come on, Judi, we've got to find them. Apparently she was a blonde girl with her hair over one eye.'

'Sandra Stubbs. But she'd never get out of the *château*, or back in. All it needs is a moat once Madame's locked us in for the night.'

'People can climb in and out of windows,' he said, and we stopped chasing up some avenue or other, like a couple of irate parents, and stared at each other. We stared and couldn't look away.

'I meant to get in touch,' he said, 'but I lost your address. Honestly.'

'You could have looked me up in the telephone book.'

'I didn't even know your second name,' he said, 'and by the time I'd got back from Greece, I'd almost forgotten what you looked like.'

'Charming,' I said, and we laughed and walked on, hand in hand.

An hour and a couple of telephone calls back to the billet which housed Guy Gerrard and his brood, and we were no nearer.

'It's a waste of time,' I said, as we searched what must have been the fiftieth café with no results.

'We're responsible for them,' Guy told me sternly, when I complained that my feet hurt. 'Don't you see?'

Well, I did see, but I couldn't see what two fourteen-year-olds could get up to in Paris, that they couldn't get up to at home, and I said so.

'You don't know Bateson,' Guy said darkly, and I began to get really worried.

And then, just as we were talking vaguely about going to the police, and in my mind's eye I was seeing the Seine being dredged, we saw them . . .

They were there on the pavement, worriedly putting together their last few coins, and arguing about how to get back. Sandra's silky hair was immaculate, falling in a long blonde sweep over a carefully made-up eye, and I relaxed.

She looked much too well groomed for someone who has just been through a fate worse than death, but Guy didn't relax. He behaved just like Mr Barrett of Wimpole Street, on one of his off days. Right there in Paris, on a warm night in spring, with the sky jammed full of stars, and the scent of chestnut blossom in the air, he told Bateson just what he thought about him.

He told him that if he had his way he would shove him on the first train out of Paris, and that if he had his way, a telegram would be sent to Bateson's father, informing him of the despicable behaviour of his son.

'We only walked about, and had a couple of drinks, sir,' Bateson said in an aggrieved tone.

'What drinks?' Guy bellowed, to the amusement of the passers-by.

'Orange,' they both said together, all outraged innocence, and Guy was the first to laugh. Then he stepped out into the road, narrowly escaping death from a coasting taxi, and handing over some paper money, put me and Sandra into it.

I had just given the driver the name of our *château*, when Guy fished in his pocket, and brought out a cigarette packet. 'I haven't got your address,' he said.

The driver started on a tuneless whistle as I groped feverishly in my handbag, and brought out a card, one of a small batch I'd had printed when the ownership of a flat had first gone to my head.

'Better take this. Cleaners' tickets tend to get handed in,' I said.

He grinned, and leaning forward, kissed me lightly on the cheek, and as the taxi shot down the boulevard with the impetus of a jet-propelled rocket, I turned round and saw him placing the card carefully in his wallet.

And the lights of Paris were beautiful, twinkling like mad as we drove away, and Sandra's eye, the one that I could see, closed itself in a cheeky wink.

'Isn't Paris *romantic*, Miss?' she said.

Have Typewriter – Will Travel

In our last year at school we were interviewed by a serious-minded youth employment officer, who tried to fit us into little slots.

'Good at biology: what about nursing?' she'd say. 'Top in maths: banking,' she'd pronounce. 'Excellent marks in cookery: domestic science?'

But when she came to me she was nonplussed. It wasn't that I was bad at everything, rather that I didn't shine at anything, and after I'd politely refused half a dozen or so of her suggestions, I could see, by the way she kept glancing at her wrist watch, that I was obviously wasting her valuable time.

She was a middle-aged lady, with pretty grey hair, and upswept spectacle frames with diamanté butterflies at their corners, which gave her round face a distinctly fairy-godmother air. I decided to be frank with her.

'Whatever I do when I leave school, it must be something adventurous,' I told her.

Her eyebrows raised themselves over the diamanté butterflies as I hastened to explain. 'What I have in mind is an unusual job, with glamour attached to it, like being au-pair girl to a foreign prince's children, or part of a pearl diver's team, or the only girl in a crew of bearded men sailing the Pacific on a raft or . . .'

I was well into my stride by now, but as I went on giving her a rough idea of what I had in mind, she took off the spectacles, and the eyes behind them were not fairy-godmotherish at all.

My voice tailed off in the middle of elaborating on my theme, and the ensuing interview with the Head-mistress was brief, but to the point. I was told that a perverted sense of humour and an over-vivid imagination might be a decided asset in some quarters, but that in the highly competitive field of employment it would get me nowhere.

The sad part about it was that no one would take me seriously. Mother went on and on about training being essential, and Father threw in a few apt remarks about qualifications being the thing. So I meekly enrolled at the local technical college for a year's intensive course in shorthand and typing, calculated to turn me into that most orthodox of beings, a private secretary.

As at school, my results were less than startling, but passably acceptable and, at the end of it all, I was given a diploma stating my speeds in shorthand, and my prowess at typing, with a few other assets such as elementary book-keeping and my dexterity with a duplicating machine thrown in.

That very day I began scanning the situations vacant columns for any big game hunter in need of a secretary to accompany him on safari, or a best-selling novelist with a villa in the South of France, requiring a secretary to type a couple of chapters a week on a balcony overlooking the Mediterranean.

There was nothing even remotely in my line, and after visiting two agencies in town, and explaining my ideas to two totally disinterested lady clerks, I hit on the idea of inserting an advertisement myself.

'Young lady, aged eighteen, willing to tackle anything unusual. Has typewriter, will travel.'

Unfortunately Father saw the draft first, and gave me a lecture on slave marketeers, dope pedlars and exploiters of an innocent girl's virtue.

I can't believe that it was only coincidence that the very next weekend at the golf club, he happened to run into a pal of his who had a friend in town in a large firm of glass manufacturers who just at that moment was scouring the whole of Middlesex for a girl with my exact potentialities.

I told myself that the interview would be experience for me when something more in my line cropped up.

As the friend of Father's friend had a slight impediment in his speech, I was able to get down the letter he dictated to me, on a king-sized electric typewriter, too. Quite good, I thought, as I wasn't really trying and had no intention of taking the job anyway.

Leaving his office I lowered myself down to street level in the splendid mahogany self-service lift, and walked through the vast entrance hall, with its pillars like slabs of frozen potted meat, out into the bright sunshine. I might as well be buried alive as work there, I told myself glumly.

Within a week I was informed on the firm's neatly headed paper that I'd got the job, and reluctantly, because being at home all day bored me to tears, and because there was nothing even remotely adventurous looming on the labour market, I decided to give it a try, merely until something more exciting came along.

The friend of the friend of my father's turned out to be the perfect boss, kind and considerate, and as he lit his pipe at least three times during the dictating of every letter, I was able to get it all down nicely. I tamed the throbbing electric typewriter into submission and settled down into what I knew was a dangerously comfortable groove.

It was a pity, I decided, that my stay with the firm was only to be a temporary one, especially after I'd met Robert Hamilton who worked two floors down in the accounts department.

Robert was definitely not my type. I knew that from the very beginning, but he was certainly attractive in a dark-suited sober kind of way. There was nothing rugged or even remotely adventurous about him. He was of medium height, brown-eyed, and when I asked him one day if he'd ever considered throwing up his job to row across the Pacific, or to become the bodyguard of a famous film star, or even to climb the Matterhorn blindfold, he looked at me as if I'd gone raving mad.

'How old are you, Gillian?' he asked kindly, leaning over my desk, his face so close to mine that I could see that his eyes weren't exactly brown but flecked with green.

'Eighteen,' I told him, my heart beating madly for some unknown reason.

He smiled. 'You'll grow up,' he told me tolerantly.

I touched the space bar of my electrically charged machine and the carriage shot across with the impetus of a jet-propelled rocket. 'Wanting to do something out of the ordinary isn't a sign of immaturity,' I told him evenly. 'If that were true, then Everest would never have been climbed, the Mayflower would never have set sail, and Sir Francis Chichester would never have completed his epic voyage.'

He wasn't impressed, but he did ask me out to dinner the following Thursday, and I accepted. It would relieve the utter boredom of my existence for one evening, I thought.

We dined at a little French restaurant where the wine costs half a crown a sip, and the menu cards are so big they could be used as wind-breaks. Robert talked well, and for someone without an ounce of pioneering spirit in his make-up, his conversation was quite interesting. He was twenty-four, he told me, as if I didn't already know, having looked him up in the office files. He lived with two bachelor friends in a flat at Richmond, and they took turns in cooking the evening meal and going to the launderette.

'We're all studying for something or other,' he went

on, 'so we don't have television, and we pick our girl-friends carefully. They must be good cooks, then in that way we can be sure of at least three square meals a week.'

Smug, I decided, as the brown eyes twinkled at me.

'Not madly exciting, I suppose,' he said.

'There's always the evening at the launderette to look forward to,' I said, and he chased an elusive prawn round his plate and grinned.

'There was the time when a duster got in the laundry bag, and we went around in yellow underpants and shirts for weeks afterwards, except old Pete who bought a bottle of bleach and used it all at one go. He went around with shredded underpants and shirts,' he went on reflectively. 'Yes, life has its moments.'

He was laughing at me, and the knowledge infuriated me. I'd be nice to him for that evening, then I'd never go out with him again. Who was he, anyway, to laugh at my dreams? Sitting opposite me in his so-correct dark suit and whiter-than-white shirt, in spite of the yellow duster? He had no soul, not even the semblance of one; no imagination, no pioneer spirit. Let him get on with his dull-as-dishwater existence and see if I cared.

Some day, I told myself, as he hailed a taxi outside the restaurant – he wasn't mean, I'd grant him that – some day I'd send him a card from the top of the Lorelei Rock. Or I might give him a passing thought as I sat with my employer in a jet aircraft, cruising at six hundred miles an hour as he dictated the odd letter umpteen thousand feet above the clouds.

Outside my gate, in the shadow of the lilac bush, Robert pulled me gently towards him. Then, holding my face still for his kiss, his mouth moved against mine, and suddenly it was as though all Heaven rocked around me.

Taken completely by surprise I moved in closer, and we clung to each other with the wonder of it all.

'You know what's happened to us, don't you?' he whispered. 'We've fallen in love. I always knew it would be like this, didn't you?'

I tried to pull away, but his kiss, tender and passionate at the same time, blurred my thoughts, and when at last we said goodnight my knees turned to water as I walked up the path.

There was no need to panic, I told myself in the weeks that followed. It was love that made promises, this was just a blind infatuation. Given time it would pass.

So I gave it time. I went out with Robert almost every evening. I even took my turn in cooking a meal at his flat. His friends swallowed it manfully, but Robert chewed each mouthful as if it were nectar from the gods – watching me across the table, always watching me with those brown eyes and sending unspoken messages of love.

I still trembled at his nearness; his ordinary pleasant face haunted my dreams, and like the heroine in a Victorian novel, I could have swooned away each time he kissed me.

He took it for granted that we would marry, and he showered my desk at the office with leaflets from estate agents. He talked about mortgages, and life insurances, and the number of children we'd have. He bought me a ring, and I wore it with a sort of guilty pride, telling myself that soon, any day now, I would find the strength to give it back to him, and tell him that marriage in a maisonette was not for me.

I considered giving up my job, moving away, anywhere out of the range of his disturbing presence. Desperately I begged him to wait a year, six months, until we were sure of each other, but each time he'd stop my words with a kiss, and the singing violins would begin their soaring music once again.

Then the firm sent round a circular explaining that they were opening a branch in Texas, and that any private secretaries interested could apply.

It wasn't quite what I'd had in mind, but there'd be scorching sun I told myself vaguely, hot winds blowing across sandy plains, corn on the cob, and blueberry pie. Away from Robert I could view the whole thing objectively, and if at the end of a year we still felt the same way about each other, then I would come back and we'd marry, and I'd settle down into the sort of domesticity I'd sworn was not for me.

I applied first, and told him afterwards. I made sure that we were in a crowded restaurant before I broke my news, with the width of a table between us, and no chance of him changing my mind with a kiss.

He heard me out in silence, a rather grim silence. 'You've actually applied?' he asked quietly, and I nodded.

'Without talking it over with me?'

I smiled nervously.

'Then there's nothing more to be said, is there?'

'Nothing,' I said bravely, trying to remember the little speech I'd prepared. 'I'll be back in a year, then if we both feel the same way we can be married straight away.'

Robert motioned to a waiter to bring the bill. 'A year is a long time,' he said coldly. 'With your adventurous inclinations you'll probably be engaged to a horse-thief by then.'

Under the fascinated gaze of the little Italian waiter I wrenched at my ring, and across the coffee cups Robert accepted it in dignified silence.

'Have your fun, Gillian,' he said as he left me at the

gate, and this time there was no kiss, no violins sending their soaring music to the dark sky.

For three whole days my anger sustained me. I had been right about him in the first place, I told myself over and over again. Smug he was, and self-opinionated, and dull. If he really loved me he would have waited. I was only eighteen, going on nineteen, I argued to myself. I hadn't even begun to live. Who did he think he was to condemn me to a life of washing nappies in a steamy maisonette?

Selfish, as well as unimaginative . . . and when I caught a glimpse of him, walking through the outer office, a sheaf of papers in his hand, I cursed my heart for beating madly and my fingers for trembling on the typewriter keys.

I was interviewed for one of the American vacancies and accepted. All the wheels were set in motion and the firm sent me leaflets extolling the beauties of Fort Worth in far-away Texas.

This was it, I told myself. This was what I had always wanted, a chance to travel to see something other than my own small corner of the world. Even my parents were enthusiastic, not realising the cause of my broken engagement, quite sure that Robert had jilted me, and that a year or so away would heal my hurt pride.

'He had a small head,' my mother said, 'and you can never trust men with small heads. Shows a meanness of disposition.'

I glared at her. Robert's head was a beautiful shape, and I should know. Hadn't I cradled it in my arms, feeling the sweetness of its weight on my breast? Hadn't I tangled my fingers in the thickness of his brown hair?'

'No ambition,' my father said, 'otherwise he'd have applied for one of the American vacancies himself. In a rut before he's thirty. I know the type.'

'Robert has still two or three years' work to do before

he becomes fully qualified,' I said coldly, and my father snorted into his newspaper.

And all the time the weeks were passing, and all the time I got more and more depressed.

Robert treated me with friendly politeness in the office, nothing more, and I lay awake at nights telling myself how unreasonable he was, then I would remember the way he'd held me close, and the way when he kissed me his brown eyes took on the dreaming look of a young child.

There was only a week to go when I caught a massive dose of chicken pox, and the firm was forced to cancel my bookings; or 'postpone' them, as they kindly said in a message from Head Office.

I lay in bed at home, and fumed and fretted, scratching myself underneath the sheets, and ignoring my mother when she told me that if I didn't stop it I'd be scarred for life.

All my friends left me severely alone, so I had plenty of time to lie and think things over in between dabbing myself with calamine lotion.

I was at my spottiest and hottest, and wearing a pair of ancient cotton pyjamas, when one evening the door-bell rang and I heard voices downstairs in the hall. I turned over on my side and closed my eyes, quite sure that no one I knew would dare to disturb my splendid isolation.

Then there were footsteps on the stairs, and my mother's voice outside my door. 'A visitor for you, dear,' she said.

I heard someone tiptoe to the bed and sit down on the little hard chair, removing my bottle of calamine lotion first.

Cautiously I opened one eye and turned over, and there was Robert, holding a cellophane-wrapped sheaf of flowers.

37

I felt a blush creep over my spots, and pulled the sheet up to my chin and blinked at him through my swollen eyelids.

'I'm highly infectious,' I said, and he said that he knew, and underneath the old cotton pyjama jacket my heart began its familiar dance.

The tenderness in his brown eyes unnerved me, and the weak tears slid down my hot cheeks. Carefully, with a corner of the sheet, he wiped them away.

'Sorry you missed your chance of high adventure,' he said, and I tried to speak through the lump in my throat, but no words came.

'They say you'll still be able to go when you're better,' he soothed. I nodded and lay quite still as his hand caressed my hair, pushing it away from my forehead.

At last I found my voice, and said what I knew I had to say. 'I love you, and I'm glad I missed going to Texas. All I want is to stay right here with you.'

But he shook his head. 'No, darling. I was wrong. You go and have your adventure, and I'll wait for you, just as you wanted me to. You can't help having itchy feet.'

Unobtrusively I scratched beneath the sheets. 'It isn't my feet that are itching,' I told him feverishly, and he laughed out loud.

'I love you,' I said again, 'and I'll marry you next week if you still want me.'

Gently he stroked my bare arm. 'The bride wore pink, an exact match to her spots,' he said, and kissed me tenderly on my flushed cheek.

When he'd gone, I lay there, scratching away happily, and dreaming rosy dreams of contentment. Love in a maisonette, and nappies hanging in the kitchen to dry. What could be more adventurous than that?

The Perfect Wife

Julie asked her mother over a wildly expensive morning telephone call: 'Did you think Peter looked all right when we came to lunch with you last Sunday?'

'Why, yes, dear,' her mother said. 'Why? Is something the matter, dear?'

Julie glanced at the newspaper in her hand. It was eleven o'clock and she'd only just found time to glance at the headlines, but one article had held her riveted as she identified with every well-chosen, rounded phrase.

'Is your husband under stress?' it asked. 'Middle thirties? Striving to keep his feet fixed on the bottom rung of the executive ladder? Worried well-nigh out of his mind by repeated redundancies, a mortgage like a millstone round his neck?

'Always aiming to be smartly dressed, on the ball, alert, keen? Showing he can hold his own against the competition of young men straight from university, whizz kids with theories on how to put a struggling firm back on its feet? Do you want to keep him alive?' the article had gone on inexorably.

'I've just realised exactly how much stress Peter has to contend with,' Julie told her mother, and went on to list the items enumerated in the article. 'It describes him exactly, and it says he should come home to the peace and quiet of a well-ordered house, with a quiet and peaceful wife waiting to greet him with a kiss and a quiet and peaceful drink.'

She sighed. 'And that's a big laugh for a start, but there's more to follow. It says he should sit down to a meal à deux by candlelight, to talk about interesting, topical subjects, with positively no office or domestic worries being aired over the fillet steak.'

'But no-one eats fillet steak nowadays, dear,' her mother interrupted. 'Not unless it's their Golden Wedding Anniversary, or they've won the Pools. Why don't you take the *Daily Wire*, dear? They don't print articles like that, but I shouldn't worry. You and Peter are young, dear, and resilient. And young people can face things you know . . .'

'I'm thirty-two and Peter is thirty-five,' Julie reminded her mother, 'and that isn't considered to be young – not these days.'

'When we were first married,' her mother was saying, 'your father was on flying operations in the war. Fourteen hours every other night over the Atlantic, searching for U-boats. In the dark. What I'm trying to say is that we faced it then, but I doubt if we could face it now.'

'Well, I don't suppose you can compare getting stuck in a traffic-jam every evening with searching for U-boats in the dark,' Julie conceded. 'And we stopped taking the *Daily Wire* because it was too big to read over breakfast. It got marmalade on it.'

'Yes,' her mother said. 'Will we be seeing you this weekend, dear? If so, I'll keep Caroline's birthday present instead of posting it. It's *soft* bricks dear, the kind she can throw at people without raising lumps. Your father says he can still feel the place where Daniel . . .'

Julie replaced the receiver with a sigh. It was all very well for her mother to refuse to take her seriously, but the article had her worried about Peter. Really worried. Take the evening before, for example. A perfectly normal evening. Junior executive under stress opens front door with his key, briefcase tucked beneath his arm, eyes starting from his head with strain of being stuck in aforementioned traffic-jam.

Dog by the name of Fido bounds up to greet him, knocking briefcase to floor, then chews straps.

Louise, gap-toothed and six and a half years old, demands immediate attention as she tells him she was top of her reading group before rotten old Miss Lacey put her up a group, which means that she is now bottom.

Daniel, aged five, rides out of the lounge on his tricycle, making revved-up engine noises, and wife of man under stress looks up briefly from stirring something in a pan, while Caroline, soon to be one year old, screams purple murder from her high-chair because she wants to get down and eat the dog's dinner, preferring it to the mashed banana on her plate.

'I thought I said no more riding round the house on that thing!' exclaims worried young executive, palely eyeing the glass dividing door with one crack already running from top to bottom.

'Mummy lets me,' says Daniel smugly, reversing with expert precision round the kitchen table, misjudging his distance badly and narrowly escaping knocking baby sister clean out of high-chair.

'Excuse me,' says Julie, scooping baby, who has now started to howl, out of the high-chair and wiping half a mashed banana from her chin.

'Rotten old Miss Lacey says I fidget,' says Louise.

'Zoom-zoom,' says Daniel, careering down the hall with the dedicated fervour of a racing driver on the last lap of the Monte Carlo Rally.

'Excuse me,' says Julie again, with rather more emphasis. 'Just watch that pan a moment while I go and put her down, Peter, there's a love.'

The article said: 'Do you want to keep your man alive?'

Putting the newspaper aside, Julie shuddered and came to a decision.

All that was yesterday. Today would be different.

Somehow, some way, she would plan her day so that when her man opened the door with his key at half-past six, there would be nothing to greet him but peace and quiet; the peace and quiet of a well-ordered household.

Unloading the washing-machine and draping the washing over the radiators to dry on account of the rain outside and the spin-dryer having gone on the blink, she made her plans with utmost care . . .

And at half-past six precisely, the house they were buying on a mortgage they couldn't afford was as still and quiet as if God had reached down His hand from the sky and told it to be still.

Caroline, Daniel and Louise had been fed, watered, bathed and shoved into their respective beds at a speed which had left their mother shaking with nervous exhaustion because of the rush.

The dog by name of Fido was sulking in the garage, lying in his basket, lop-ears dangling over the side, with brown eyes rolled upwards as if asking the meaning of it all.

The table in the dining-room was set for two, half-way burned down Christmas candles at the ready; Christmas-present tablemats depicting Favourite Constable Paintings set in place; a casserole of braising steak – which should have been fillet but wasn't on account of the breathtaking price – sitting on the middle shelf in the oven.

Julie wore an outfit she'd worn before Caroline was born but never since. It seemed to make her bulge in the middle, and her eyelids were a strange greenish blue, the result of Louise using her eye-shadow as an artist's palette the day before.

She stared at herself in the mirror in the hall. Was it really so long since she had tarted herself up when they weren't having a baby-sitter and going out? No wonder she couldn't remember the last time her stressful husband had said that he loved her to distraction . . .

And so, when she greeted him with a warm, loving and welcoming kiss, almost before he had had a chance to wrench his key from the door, he stared at her in undisguised horror. 'Just because I forgot our wedding anniversary, it doesn't mean the thought wasn't there,' he said, putting the briefcase down and looking round curiously for the dog by the name of Fido.

Gently Julie shook her head.

'Your birthday?'

Again the sweet denial.

'My birthday?'

She smiled and kissed him again, longer this time.

'Something you can only tell me when the stage is set?' he asked, going through and eyeing the candlesticks, the Constable placemats and then staring at her slightly bulging waistline with a look of complete horror on his face.

Julie gave him a calm and peaceful smile, and pushing him down into his chair, passed him a calm and peaceful drink.

'Just unwind, darling, while I dish up,' she said. 'Forget what's happened at the beastly office today; forget what the Managing Director said at that beastly Management Conference, and in five minutes I'll call you through.'

'But I've been promoted. With a rise if things look up,' he said, following her, glass in hand, and staring round the silent, childless kitchen in bewilderment.

'They're okay, aren't they?' he asked, his eyes slewing up to the ceiling.

'Perfectly okay, darling,' Julie assured him. 'Sound asleep in their beds.' All being well, she added to herself. She bent down to the cooker to check on the braising, that should have been fillet, steak and felt the

43

side zip of her dress strain at its prongs. She groaned to herself, and vowed to diet – as from tomorrow.

'This is the way it's going to be from now on, darling, during the week when you've been running in that beastly rat-race. They'll be tucked up in bed, with luck asleep, by the time you're home, so you can relax and unwind quietly.

'Now go and change into something more comfortable and finish your drink, and I'll call you in a minute.'

And in between straining the cauliflower and mashing the carrots, she found time to dash upstairs and comfort the screaming baby, and to hiss a dire warning through the door of the older children's bedroom.

Surely, she wondered, as she flew back into the kitchen, Daniel wasn't sitting on top of the wardrobe? From that one swift glance it had seemed to be so but she must have been imagining things. It was impossible . . .

'All ready, darling,' she called in a serene and soothing voice. Then, as the refugee from the rat-race came into the dining-room, she lit the candles and the room was filled with a soft glow.

Julie snuggled up next to Peter for a few moments before she served the special dinner, designed to relax the junior executive under stress.

'We won't be able to afford wine every evening, of course,' she said later, holding her glass high. 'But it's nice every now and then, isn't it?'

Peter nodded through a mouthful of braising, that should have been fillet, steak. But he didn't look very happy.

'Didn't they want to hear another episode of the bedtime story I'm telling them? It's really quite good. I was making it up as I drove home in the car.' He sounded disappointed.

'I read them a story,' Julie soothed. 'About Johnny and Jane visiting the zoo.'

Her husband toyed with a bit of unmashed carrot that had somehow got away.

'But they can't bear Johnny and Jane. I'm telling them this story where we all go to live on a desert island and we tame this gorilla, and it wheels Caroline about in a pram hollowed out of the trunk of a tree.'

He held his fork half-way to his mouth.

'Isn't that the baby crying? Maybe if I just went up and tucked her in more firmly . . . ?'

His glance over the flickering candles held more than a hint of pleading in it. But his wife ignored it. 'I started to read a book today,' she continued, smiling firmly. 'Well, I only had time to read the blurb on the jacket when I was in the library, but it's about this couple who stow away in a space capsule and live on the moon, so that they can see the earth in-depth, if you see what I mean.'

The stressful young executive looked a little perplexed.

She put her elbows on the table and cupped her chin in her hands, the way she had seen the after-dinner mint hostess do on television.

'They feel that by going so far away they can get things into perspective,' she went on. 'See how petty are our motivations, how earthbound our silly, scheming lives . . . They . . .'

'That is the baby screaming,' Peter said, throwing down his napkin and leaping up from the table, 'and from the way the light-fitting is swaying about, I would say that Daniel has already started training for the British Olympics team.'

And before Julie could stop him, he was half-way upstairs . . .

And it turned out that the baby just loved the spicy

lemon mousse which Julie had taken almost an hour to make. And there was enough of the casserole left to fill two small side-plates for Daniel and Louise and they tucked in greedily.

Their mother wondered, just for a moment, what it would do to their stomachs, mixed in with their fish-finger tea, but she had to admit they did look lovely sitting up at the table in their night-clothes, with the candlelight shining on their clean faces and tangling in the softness of their hair.

Then, with the baby perched on his knee, the man of stress, looking relaxed for the first time since he'd put his key in the door, lowered his voice dramatically and continued with the story he had been inventing.

'And this whale, coming in from the sea, had legs and could walk. "Good-evening," it said in a deep and rumbling voice. "Tonight we will dance on the beach and eat candy-floss coral." '

'Go on, Dad,' said Daniel excitedly, cheeks bulging with roasted potato.

'Then what did it say, Daddy?' demanded Louise, blue eyes round with delight.

'Da-da,' said Caroline, and with a hand liberally coated with spicy lemon mousse, stroked her father's cheek.

And smiling at her, the man of stress continued: ' "I can promise you all," said the whale, picking up a tree and biting off a piece as if it were a stick of celery, "I can promise you all that we will have a whale of a time . . ." '

Julie spoke softly to herself: 'I think we'll change back to the *Daily Wire* . . .'

Are You Listening Miranda?

That evening, Janet told herself firmly as she climbed the four flights of stairs to her room, she would be so busy that the hours to be got through before she could go to bed would pass like a flash.

She would make herself a corn omelette, then she would wash her hair, and *iron* it to get rid of those horrible kinks! She would use the precious shillings stored in a beer glass on the mantelpiece, and have the gas-fire on at full blast all the time. She would draw the curtains against the driving rain, and after she'd finished washing and ironing her hair she would write to her mother.

She might even start that knitted dress already cast on its poker needles. She would knit furiously to see if the instructions lived up to their claim that it could be knitted in a couple of evenings. She would do some washing and festoon it over the sink and tomorrow, as someone had once said, would be another day . . .

To give in to this utter and aching loneliness after three weeks of living alone, was sheer defeatism. She would make friends in time. One of these days she would ask one of the other secretaries at work to come round for a coffee. It would be as simple as that.

Breathless, she reached her own landing. 'I really ought to get up just ten minutes earlier,' she said aloud in a conversational tone as she closed the door behind her. 'Then I could make the bed and tidy round a bit, and it wouldn't look like this when I come in.'

Straightening the covers of the divan, she rescued a large rag doll from the floor, and placed it on the pillow.

'Just listen to that rain, Miranda,' she said. 'Maybe I won't bother with the corn, or the omelette for that matter. A boiled egg will do, and perhaps an apple afterwards. Did you hear what I said, Miranda?'

The doll stared back at her with embroidered, vacant eyes, its rag-stuffed legs splayed out over the candle-wick bedspread, and after she had put a pan of water on to boil, Janet peeled off her mud-splashed tights, slipped out of her short skirt and skinny sweater, and reached for her flower-printed housecoat.

'Woman in a dressing-gown. That's me, Miranda. And just you look at this towel. Sordid isn't the word. Hope the eye-liner marks come off at the launderette. Tomorrow morning I'm going there, and while my washing's revolving round and round, I'm going to the supermarket on the corner. *He* might be there.'

Sitting down suddenly on the bed, she tweaked the doll's button nose. 'You know who I mean, stupid. I came straight back and told you about him. We were both wandering about with those silly wire baskets, staring at the biscuits, and we reached for the same packet at the same time. Shortbreads they were. We got talking, and he told me he had come down here after his final year at university, and this was his first job. He had a beard, a ginger one, and I don't like ginger beards, or beards, but there was something about his eyes. They were kind . . .

'I wonder if I ought to have given him my actual address when he asked me where I lived? I should have said: Top floor flat, 34a Ashbury Gardens, not just Ashbury Gardens. Do you realise he might have called to see us? He might have actually climbed the stairs and rung our bell.'

Then suddenly she was still, her whole body stiffened into the concentration of listening.

There was somebody coming up the stairs. There was somebody pausing outside the door . . . Then they walked away, and she heard the burr of the bell on the next door.

'Honestly!' she said out loud. 'Why should I think he'd have given me a thought? Why should I think he would go around like some grotty old detective picking up clues to try and find me again? I bet he doesn't know whether my hair is dark or fair, or whether I'm fat or thin or medium.'

She started walking restlessly round the room and then picking up the doll, she swung it briefly by its orange satin skirt. 'I think he was shy.'

She dropped the doll back on the pillow. 'Well, that makes two of us.'

She had forgotten all about the pan, and now it had boiled almost dry, and the egg was bullet-hard. For a minute she considered throwing it away in the pedal-bin underneath the tiny sink, then she changed her mind.

'You don't stop feeling hungry, no matter what, Miranda. The more lonely you are, the more hungry you are. Honestly. That's why fat people are often unhappy and not jolly like they're supposed to be.'

Stretching out her hand she switched on her portable radio, and a blurred voice reciting a sad-sounding poem made her switch quickly over to another wave length. There was a faint echo of music as if it came from far away, and she remembered that the battery was flat.

'I'll get one tomorrow,' she told the doll.

It was as she dried her hair, the hum of the hand dryer shutting out the sound of the rain, that she started to think about her mother; without meaning to, just as if she'd switched on the thoughts like she'd switched on the radio, but this time the words were loud and clear.

'No, I don't understand,' her mother had said. 'I don't understand, and I never will. I could perhaps understand if we were always having rows or some-

49

thing, or if you'd got a job to go to in London, but just to pack up and go – a young girl like you – why, anything could happen to you. Men lie in wait for girls like you, arriving at London stations. I saw a programme about it on the television, and I don't believe that secretaries get paid as much as that. Goodness gracious me, your father doesn't get much more than that . . .'

By allowing her mind to wander, Janet had dismissed the loud complaining voice to a whisper. She had sat there, and dreamed of the time when she would be free. Free to be herself; to eat when she liked, to stay up all night if she wanted to; to come in and know there would be no-one there to question her, to pry, to query her every movement.

Where have you been? And why must you wear your hair like that, covering half your face? And why don't you join something? The local Dramatic Society or the Youth Club? When I was your age I was always in something . . .

She had sat there, her fringe tangling with her eyebrows, her hair falling fine and pale, almost to her waist. She had sat there, imagining the room she would rent in far-away London when she was free. She saw it transformed with her posters on the walls, her outsized doll, Miranda, sprawled decoratively across the divan bed. She saw the gaily coloured rug she would buy with her first week's wages, the set of coffee mugs, the friends who would come round, the parties she would give.

And she had won. The questions stopped, but they were there, in her mother's eyes, a perpetual and sad reproach.

'How d'you think I'd look with my hair on top?' she asked the doll quite seriously, and for the next ten minutes she tried it this way and that in front of the dressing-table mirror.

'I don't believe it's only half-past eight,' she said aloud. 'It can't be only half-past eight.'

Kneeling on the bed she propped up the doll in a sitting position, its long, boneless back supported by the pillow.

'It's Friday night, Miranda. And this is swinging London, the place where it all happens. Are you listening, Miranda? Only a short bus ride away from here, there are people, hundreds and hundreds of people, walking along crowded pavements, holding hands. There are shops lit up in Oxford Street, and Regent Street, and restaurants to go into out of the rain. There are theatres and lights, and coffee bars, and people, and traffic. Are you listening, Miranda?'

To her horror her voice wobbled on the verge of lost control, and as she buried her face in the doll's neck, her hair fell forward, sweet smelling and milk pale, covering her face . . .

It was at that exact moment that the boy turned away from the door, shrugging his shoulders, and starting back down the four flights of stairs.

There was someone else in there with her. He might have known she wasn't the kind of girl to spend her evenings alone. It had been a stupid thing to do anyway, going to all that trouble to find out exactly where she lived.

He trailed one hand down the banister rail. He didn't go much anyway for that type of girl. Soft straight hair, hiding a face not so much pale as transparent; but there had been something about her eyes, a kind look, a lost look he had immediately recognised.

Down in the hall he turned his head and looked back up the long winding stairs. For a few moments he hesitated.

So what if there was someone in there with her? Someone she was talking to with such animation? He could have made some excuse, pretended he'd come to

51

the wrong door, pretended he'd known the person who'd lived there before.

But he was no good at that kind of thing. No good with the glib smooth talk and the easy lie.

And out in the street the rain still fell, relentlessly, bouncing back off the pavement, and his ginger hair was already wet through, plastered in soft curls down his neck.

As he turned up the collar of his jacket he glanced at his watch. 'It can't be only nine o'clock,' he said aloud to himself in a conversational tone before he walked slowly away.

Mr Fix-It

Being what was once called a helpless female had been
no deterrent to my pipping three men at the post for
my job as reporter on the local paper. Or to living by
myself in a flat at the top of a tall Victorian house. But
when it came to unbunging a bunged-up sink, I was
about as much use as an early-nineteenth-century hero-
ine having herself the vapours.

I stared at the swirling dirty water in dismay. I
opened the cupboard door underneath the sink and
tried again to turn the handle, which I vaguely knew
should release the troubled waters into the bucket I
had placed below. Nothing happened.

I said a word that would never have been allowed
to appear in the article I was writing at the moment,
and went to get help.

I hadn't met the occupants of the flat below, but a
tall man answered my ring, and grinned down at me.

'Not to worry, Phyllis. I'll be up in a tick.' He disap-
peared for a minute and came back with what he called
an adjustable spanner.

'Everyone should have one, Phyllis,' he told me,
leaping ahead up the stairs, and in two minutes flat he
had done the necessary, dislodged whatever had been
the obstruction, and bowed deep.

'How long has that plate-rack been hanging lop-
sided?' he wanted to know, as he wiped his hands on
a kitchen towel. 'Tell you what, Phyllis, I'm going out
now, late already as a matter of fact, but I'll come up
tomorrow and put it right.'

'My name is Harriet, and thank you very much,' I
said, but with a flash of extraordinary white teeth he

was gone, telling me over his shoulder that all the girls he met were called Phyllis until he got to know them better.

The flat seemed very empty when he had gone. He was a big man, bounding with energy. He had thick black hair springing back into a wide forehead, and smiling dark-blue eyes.

Strangely he seemed to have left some of his vitality behind him, so that I acknowledged to myself for the first time since leaving home that I was lonely.

I had a deeply fulfilling job, a few girl friends with whom I occasionally went to restaurants, plays and the ballet, and that seemed enough. But now I stared at my solitary lamb chop in dismay, and found myself wondering where the tall young man was spending his evening.

Was it with a Phyllis, or with a girl he knew well enough to call by her real name?

It should not have mattered – but, ridiculously, it did.

I was so busy the next day that normally I would have stayed on in my office, but remembering his promise I bundled up the article I was working on and took it home.

A bitter cold flurry of rain sprayed down from the winter sky, and I tucked the big envelope safely underneath my mohair poncho as I walked to the tube station. It would, I told myself, be unthinkable if I was out when he called.

'That's better, Phyllis,' he said, when the plate-rack that had so offended his eye was in position. 'It must have driven you mad slewing to one side like that.'

'I honestly hadn't noticed it,' I told him. Then, when he turned to go, I took a deep breath and asked if he had eaten.

He shrugged his shoulders. 'Well, no. The two bods

I share with are out on the town, and I was just going to make myself a baked bean butty.'

'A what?' I had to laugh, but he assured me that there was nothing to beat it.

'Just slosh a heap straight from the tin, slap on the lid, and that's that.'

I took another deep breath. 'Look . . . er . . . ?'

'Fergus.'

'Fergus. I've got a casserole in the oven. Tuna fish, mushrooms, potatoes and tomatoes. There's enough for two if you would like to stay.'

Within minutes I was handing him a can of beer from the fridge and turning up the oven to hurry along the browning of the casserole, which wasn't *quite* as ready as I had made it out to be.

And by the time we had eaten we had found out quite a lot about each other . . .

I told him about my job and how I did not mind working hard because it was all I have ever wanted to do since leaving university, and he told me that he was an accountant, newly chartered with a local firm.

'Did you always want to work with figures?' I asked as I made two mugs of instant coffee and carried them through into my tiny sitting-room. 'My electric percolator has gone on the blink,' I explained as I put the mugs down on a low table.

Fergus handed me a packet of small cigars, and when I shook my head, he asked me did I mind, before lighting one himself.

'I was really pushed into accountancy, and though I enjoy it now my real ambition was to do something quite different,' he said, leaning back in his chair, his blue eyes serious.

'You see here a man who only wants to please. I was a boy who could use a hammer before he knew what to do with a teething ring. I could string together a model aeroplane quicker than some of my pals could open the packet. I was a boy who loved to use his hands.' He spread them wide, and I leaned forward, intrigued.

'My parents, my father in particular, wanted me to have what they called a white-collar job. They had me when they were in their mid-forties, Phyllis, and they thought a job where a man gets his hands dirty was not for their only son.

'Their ambition was for me to go to an office in a dark suit and with a tie neatly knotted over a spanking white shirt. So when they gave me my first car as an incentive I went along with them, studying by day and diving underneath that old banger every evening, taking her to pieces, just for the joy of putting her together again.'

I was enraptured. Fergus was baring his soul, and I held my breath waiting for him to go on, when I noticed that his beautiful eyes had taken on a glazed look. He had obviously lost the thread of what he was telling me.

'Did you say that your coffee percolator was broken?' He jumped up from his chair. 'Let me have a look at it, Phyllis. There might be some little thing that just needs adjusting.'

It was past eleven when he went, flushed with triumph, with the merry sound of the electric coffee jug perking away like mad. I felt I had to drink two full mugs in his honour, and was kept awake most of the night as my thoughts whirled round in my head like a moth caught in a light fitting.

A strange evening, with no work done, but when he left me Fergus had cupped my face with his hands and kissed me goodnight.

'See you, Harriet,' he said.

I suppose it sounds funny, really. I mean, there are men who can live quite happily with the sound of a creaking door for their entire married life; there are wives who have to kick the spin-dryer four times to get it vibrating; but by the time I had known Fergus for two months everything in my flat spun and whirled to perfection.

He had relaid the carpet because he said the pile was going in the wrong direction, he had lowered my writing table, then raised my writing chair to ensure that my elbows were in the right typing position. He had screwed down every loose surface with such verve that I might have been living on the top deck of a schooner in a force-ten gale.

I learnt how not to tell him when my bedside lamp switched itself on when it should have been off, or when something went wrong with my toaster, but one thing I did not learn, and that was how to stop loving him.

He admitted that he loved me too, then just as I was surfacing from one of his kisses he noticed that there was a knot in the fine gold chain I wear round my neck, and the beautiful moment was over.

Have you ever tried discussing wedding plans with a man whose eyes are meeting at the bridge of his nose as he picks away with your eyebrow tweezers at a length of fine gold chain?

I took him to visit my parents, and I could see that they were all set to love him as well, especially my father, who for as many years as I could remember had spent three hours trying to get the lawn mower to kick into action, then ten minutes actually cutting the grass. Fergus put it right in a morning.

'My vacuum cleaner doesn't pick up as it should,' my mother told me wistfully, and I quelled her with a glance. Then, as we left them at the door, Fergus remembered that we had knocked instead of ringing the bell, and we stayed for another two hours whilst he fixed the bell-push.

'Fergus the Fixer', I called him nastily on the long drive home. Then because I was tired, and he was listening for a mythical knock in the car engine instead of listening to me, I told him I could never dream of marrying him as we were totally incompatible.

'It sounds as if it might be coming from the boot,' said Fergus, and there, nigh on midnight in a cold and dark lay-by, he stopped the car and went round the back to investigate.

On the landing outside my door I told him that I never ever wanted to set eyes on him again.

'There's no point in you coming up any more, because everything is working at the moment,' I told him coldly, then I left him standing there with amazement writ large on his nice face.

And the very next day, our local poet, on whom I'd once written a feature, asked me out to dinner. He was liquid-eyed, with long flowing hair, and I accepted without a moment's hesitation.

At least Owen Greatrex would not know the difference between a screwdriver and a soup ladle, I told myself, and I was right.

Owen took me to a Greek restaurant dotted with rude statues, and over our moussaka he told me that my eyes were silver-light. He passed me the salt without even noticing that the top was loose, and when we got into his car the engine sounded as though a thousand paper clips were whirling round inside, but he didn't turn a hair of his flowing locks.

As I stood with him on the landing outside my door I could see Fergus's face peering up at us through a slit in the banisters.

'Oh, but you must come in, Owen,' I heard myself say in a false voice, when it looked as if my little poet was going to back away. And when the door of the flat below banged to with a crash that shook the old house to its foundations, I should have been well pleased.

But of course I wasn't. I made two gorgeous mugs of coffee, in the smoothly working percolator; then, as we sipped together in a kind of melancholy companionship, Owen took a slip of paper from his top pocket and placed a pair of half-moon spectacles on his hawklike nose.

'This is my latest, Harriet,' he told me sorrowfully, and solemnly started to read.

The poem was all about a man who, in the space of one day, loses his job, is mugged on the way home, and then, when he finally gets there, finds a note from his girl friend to say that all is completely over between them.

He then goes out to the garage to hang himself, and lo, there on the path is a dirty great pool of oil with the moonlight shimmering on it. He stares down at it, and lo, he discovers that all that matters is there, in the glory of that moonlit oil. Forgotten are his troubles as he realises that faced with such unexpected beauty his life is worth living after all.

'It's surprising how different we all are,' I said, and Owen raised his eyebrows over the ridiculous spectacles.

'We are?'

I nodded. 'Fergus's troubles would have been mitigated by that patch of oil too, but not because of the moonlight. He would have gone right back into the house for a packet of detergent and an old shirt to wipe up the mess. Yes, that would have been enough to set Fergus's adrenalin flowing again. He has a practical turn of mind, you see.'

Owen put the poem away. 'Was that Fergus's dark glowering face I saw glaring up at us from the landing below?'

I nodded again, and Owen got up to go. 'Then I'd better be off. Do you think I'll be safe on the way down?'

'If he does bob out and bonk you one it will only be with an adjustable spanner,' I told him, and I went to bed with one ear cocked to the telephone in case it should happen to ring.

And of course the only way to end would be to tell you that I broke something, or fused the lights, anything for an excuse.

But this is 1980, not 1908, and liberated career girls have no need to run after men. They are self-sufficient, a law to themselves, and of course all that jazz went out decades ago.

However, after a week of silence I could stand it no more, so one cold dark night, with the rain flinging itself in fury at my window, I put down the article I was reading, and with all thoughts of my liberated, 1980 career-girl image vanishing fast, I went and knocked hesitantly at Fergus's door.

He stood there before me, aged ten years since I last saw him, with anguish staring from his vivid blue eyes.

'Yes?' he said.

'Something needs mending,' I said straight out, and with a sigh he went for his spanner and followed me upstairs.

'What is it?' he asked, standing on the rug in front of my electric fire, as pale and shaken as no man has any right to be.

I took a deep breath, and with a gesture that would have done any Victorian heroine proud, I placed a hand over my genuinely heaving bosom.

'My heart,' I said clearly. 'I can't go on without you, Fergus, that's all.'

He was by my side in one bound, pulling me into his arms, holding me tight, kissing my eyes, my throat, then my mouth with such sweetness I felt I could die of it and float up to heaven on the spot.

'I'll have that put right in less than a tick,' he said, then he lowered his head and kissed me again.

The Gentle Man

When the telephone rang Mary was sure that it would be her mother-in-law with her usual list of Friday shopping. So sure, that as she said hello, her free hand was groping in the drawer of the hall table for paper and pencil. But it was a man's voice, deep and hesitant. 'Is that . . . is that you, Mary?'

She recognised his voice straight away, and her heart turned right over. 'Yes, it's me.'

She could feel his hesitation, and she imagined him sitting at his desk, his long hand with the tapering fingers holding the receiver.

'This is Stephen Marland,' he said. 'I thought . . . I thought I'd just like to say how very much I enjoyed meeting you last night.'

Mary sat down on the little chair beside the phone. 'Yes it was nice.'

'Nice'. A word she used far too often according to Robert.

'I was thinking,' the voice went on. 'It's a long time, a whole year, before the next Annual Dinner and somehow, this morning, a year seems an awful long time to wait before I see you again . . . I was wondering, that is, I was thinking, would you like to have lunch with me one day next week?'

Mary pushed nervously at her hair. 'Lunch?' she said, as if the simple word was one she couldn't comprehend. 'Oh, that would be nice.'

And again she heard Robert's mocking voice: 'The scenery's nice, the house is nice, the food is nice. Is that the full extent of your vocabulary, woman?'

'Wonderful,' the voice at the other end of the wires

61

said. 'Shall we make it Tuesday, then?' And he named a well-known West End restaurant, and suggested a time, and she said that would be fine, and he said how very much he was looking forward to it, then they said goodbye, and the telephone went dead.

As if in a daze, Mary replaced the receiver and went back to what she'd been doing. At least she started to go back to what she'd been doing, but she'd forgotten what it was.

So she went and sat at the kitchen table, with her hands clasped on the red, formica-topped counter, and stared at the wall with its washable, kitchen-utensil printed paper, and saw absolutely nothing.

All right then. She was Mary Edwards, thirty-nine years old. Not an old woman, but a long way from being young. She was a good stone overweight for her height, she was twenty years' married and the mother of two grown-up children, and a man had just rung her up and asked her for a date.

She sat there, quite still, trying to take it in . . .

Her head ached a little, the way it always did when she had drunk too much wine the night before, and although the hairdresser had arranged her hair beautifully the previous afternoon, backcombing it slightly and then smoothing it into an attractive shape, now it looked a mess – well if not exactly a mess, just plain dull and ordinary, like herself.

Mary Edwards, who had only known one man in her life. Robert, who had courted and married her within three months of their first meeting, and to whom she had been faithful, never even questioning her fidelity for twenty long years.

'Oh, Lord,' she said out loud, and in the silence of her blue and white kitchen the words startled her. 'I'll make myself a cup of tea,' she said, and switched the kettle on, and sat down again and watched it absorbed, waiting passively for it to come to the boil.

But inside her head she was carrying on a silent conversation with herself . . . It was 1970, wasn't it? And a man could take a woman out to lunch, talk to her, and what did that signify? Nothing.

When Robert came in that evening she would greet him gaily with: 'What do you think? Stephen Marland rang me this morning and asked me to have lunch with him next Tuesday. No, honestly. He did. Quite a laugh, isn't it?'

And Robert would say: 'What, that old fuddy-duddy? Didn't think he had it in him. Are you going?'

She'd shrug her shoulders. 'Might as well. I have some shopping to do, anyway. I'll be able to kill two birds with one stone.'

They'd laugh, and talk about something else, as if what she'd said was of no importance whatever . . .

Biting her lip, Mary walked across to the wall cupboard, and took down a cup and saucer. She wouldn't tell Robert, and if she did his reaction would be – she poured a stream of water into the teapot, then saw that she'd forgotten to put in the tea – the truth was she didn't know what Robert's reaction would be.

Anger? Jealousy? No, to be jealous one had to be in love, passionately in love, and she had known that Robert had stopped loving her passionately a long time ago.

He was fond of her, even though she irritated him most of the time. When they were first married her prettiness had more than made up for her lack of education; it was only since Robert had 'got on' that her inability to make light conversation, her ignorance of what he called the 'form', had made him a little impatient with her.

'Why don't you make an effort?' he had asked. 'Take a course in poise – there are plenty to choose from.'

But the very thought of practising walking and speech-making in front of those hordes of young, self-assured, would-be model girls terrified her.

Once, about a year ago, she'd looked across the room at him as he watched television, slumped well down in his chair. 'Do you love me?' she'd said, surprising herself.

But he'd been half asleep, and he'd blinked and screwed his head round, and said: 'Did you say something?' And she'd said it was nothing, and he'd asked wasn't it coffee time, and that had been that.

Gavin and Gillian had been born, but as far as love went, that didn't signify anything – babies could be conceived with lust, with habit, or even boredom. She knew that, too.

Sighing, she took the cup of tea to the table and sat down again.

Then, last night, at the Annual Dinner and Dance of Robert's firm, as the wife of the general manager, she'd had to make a speech, the first public speech she'd made in her life. It had weighed on her mind for weeks.

First she'd written it down, then she'd learnt it off by heart, and all through the five-course dinner she'd hardly tasted a thing.

Never able to trust her own dress sense, for weeks she'd studied fashion magazines, and digested the fact that, with a plain, well-cut dress, a woman couldn't go wrong, but next to the other women in their smart blacks and sequined bosoms, her dress had looked what she suspected it was. Plain drab.

Perhaps if Robert had said, 'You look nice, darling . . .' No, not *nice*, nice was her word – if he'd said, 'You're looking lovely tonight, darling,' then she would have felt she was lovely.

But he hadn't said a word; just asked her to straighten his bow-tie, then reminded her that there'd be a microphone, and told her the correct distance to stand away from it . . .

She jumped as the man on her left said something to her, and apologising, turned round and looked straight into a pair of twinkling brown eyes, set below a thatch of black hair.

'I'm so sorry,' she said. 'I was day-dreaming.'

He smiled at her. 'Speeches should be made before dinner, not after. I guessed what you were thinking about, but there's no need to worry, really.'

Unable to resist the temptation, she undid the clasp of her evening bag to check that her notes were still there. She tried to think of her opening words, but her mind was a formless blank. A waiter hovered at her side refilling her glass of wine, and she raised it and drank deeply.

'Sometimes it's better to speak off the cuff,' he said, but she shook her head in disagreement.

'Oh no, that way I couldn't think of a thing. I've written it all down and learnt it. I even taped it and played it back on my son's tape-recorder, and now it's all gone.'

Under cover of her table-napkin, she took out the scrap of paper, and reassured herself with the first few words, and as the fish course came round she was silently mouthing them to herself . . .

The man on her left spoke again, and she found that she'd forgotten his name. He was new to the firm, the chief accountant, a man of integrity, Robert had said . . . what was his name? Stuart? Stephen? Yes, that was it. Stephen Marland.

'They're only people, you know,' he said suddenly, 'and when this is over they'll go home to their own lives, their own problems, their own heaven or hell.'

She smiled politely and bit her lip. What was it Robert had told her about him? Furrowing her brow, she tried to remember. His wife had died, leaving him with a son to bring up, and now the son had left university and gone to Canada to do research there, and he would be all alone. Sympathy made her forget her own anxiety for a moment.

'You must be feeling very lonely now that your son has gone away, Mr Marland,' she said.

He fingered the stem of his wine glass and she noticed that his fingers were long and slim, and the nails beautifully kept.

Yes,' he said, and his direct honesty surprised and intrigued her again. 'Yes, I am lonely, and the name is Stephen, by the way. But David really left home the day he went to university, and I would not want to encroach on his life. I did not want him to grow up guilt-ridden because he had always to think about me. I weaned him away from me as far as I could, a long time ago.'

'That was a brave thing to do,' she said, and he smiled at her.

'We can all be brave when we care enough, and might I say how that dress becomes you, Mrs Edwards? That creamy shade is exactly right for you. Soft and feminine.'

The wine was going to her head, and she laughed out loud. 'Mary's the name, and I'm glad you like my dress. The assistant in the shop said that it was 'just me' and that didn't help at all, because I've never been the kind of person who knows what 'just me' is, if you understand what I mean?'

Gravely he said, 'I know just what you mean,' and she glanced at him to see if he was laughing at her, but he was perfectly serious.

'You're very kind,' she said, and for an insane moment she had an irresistible urge to touch him, to run her fingers down the sleeve of his dinner jacket. 'I shouldn't drink wine really. I haven't a good head for wine.'

From her other side Robert was nudging her, and showing her the beautifully produced programme. 'You come after the Loyal Toast,' he whispered, 'and don't forget what I told you about the microphone. Close, but not too close, and if they laugh, wait before you carry on, and when they present you with the watch, try to look surprised . . .'

Immediately the sense of panic rose again, blurring her vision and making her heart beat in dull, heavy thuds in her chest. She stared down in horror at the over-large steak being lowered on to her plate by the hovering waiter. How was she going to eat that? As she murmured her thank you, she looked round the big room and calculated that there must have been at least three hundred people there, all busy plying knives and forks, laughing and talking.

She imagined all those anonymous faces turned towards her, and once again her fingers groped and found the catch of her evening bag. 'Ladies and Gentlemen . . .' No, that wasn't the way Robert had told her she must start. She opened the bag and her fingers tightened on the folded paper.

'Tell me about yourself, Mary,' Stephen said. 'I believe you have two children? Am I right?'

'I've forgotten what I'm going to say,' she said.

He passed her the mustard. 'French or English?'

'English would be nice,' she said, and she watched his long fingers, mesmerised, as he piled a little mound on the side of her plate. She began to feel sick.

'How old are they?' he was asking, and she forced herself to reply.

'Gillian is eighteen, and Gavin is sixteen now.'

'At school?'

She nodded. 'Gillian's the clever one. She's going up to Oxford, but Gavin is just a plodder. He tries hard, but he isn't the academic type, and that's all there is to it. Robert is disappointed that it isn't the other way round. He says it's unfair that the girl should have all the brains.'

Turning her head she saw that Robert was half-way through his steak, and she forced herself to take a mouthful. 'Gavin is like me, a dunderhead, and Gillian is like Robert. In looks too. That's funny, isn't it?'

'I'd like to meet Gavin,' Stephen said. 'He sounds nice.'

As he spoke, Mary thought about her son, small for his age, never looking quite clean, consistently in the bottom half of his form list, bringing home end-of-term reports that Robert tossed aside in disgust.

But the last time she'd been to the school Open Day, his form-master had said: 'I don't think Gavin has a single enemy in the whole school. His maths are impossible, and his English is worse, but to know your son is to like him.'

To know your son is to like him ... Mary tasted the sound of the words on her tongue and smiled.

'That's better,' the man on her left said. 'And I wouldn't worry if I were you about finishing off that enormous steak. I've just been looking at the menu, and we're having a Baked Alaska, whatever that is.'

'Baked Alaska,' Mary said, 'is an ice-cream sweet that you bake in the oven. It's funny, isn't it, to think of baking ice-cream?' She told him about the time Robert had invited an important client and his wife to dinner and, trying to impress, she'd made one, but when the time came she was so petrified in case the ice-cream had melted, that she hadn't dared to open the oven door.

'And had it?' Stephen asked gravely, and she told him that, much to her surprise, it was perfect.

He asked her how it was done and she told him, and he listened, nodding his head now and again, as if he were going to go straight home and make one himself.

'Do you cook for yourself?' she asked him over coffee, accepting a cigarette, and he shook his head.

'I have a midday meal out, and a Mrs Thing who comes in twice a week in the afternoons and cleans and leaves me a casserole in the oven.'

She sipped her liqueur and laughed. 'A Mrs Thing?'

He grinned. 'There have been so many of them and I can't possibly remember their names, so I just call all of them Mrs Thing.'

As they talked the microphone was being set up, and before Mary had time to give way to panic again the Loyal Toast was proposed, and it was time for her speech.

After the first few seconds, when her voice sounded high-pitched and entirely unlike her own, she carried on without having to refer to her notes once. She said the line that she had thought was only mildly funny but, replete with good food and wine, the entire room laughed, and remembering what Robert had said, she waited, composed, for the laughter to stop before she carried on.

Stephen had been right. They were only people, and when amid applause she sat down, it was he who whispered his congratulations.

Robert said nothing, but she could tell he was pleased, and when the music started he asked her to dance.

'Dancing with you is like taking a walk backwards,' she'd once teased him, and as they progressed on their uneventful way round the room, she mentioned the speech.

'Was it all right?'

'Just the job, love,' Robert said, but even as he spoke he was trying to attract the attention of a man of

69

elephantine proportions, dancing with his wife who wore a dress hung with glass bugles which shivered in rhythm as they danced.

'Old Renshawe,' Robert whispered. 'Must have a word with him after this. A do like this is a good opportunity for chatting up the staff I don't see every day . . .'

Mary smiled and said that she understood. When the music started again it was a slow fox-trot, and Stephen came over to her. With old-fashioned courtesy he asked for the pleasure of the next dance.

Their steps matched perfectly; as his arm tightened round her, she felt happiness light as a bubble inside her, and decided that she'd definitely drunk too much wine.

'I've drunk too much wine,' she told him.

With his face serious and intent, he looked at her. 'I can see it sparkling in your eyes,' he said, and when the music stopped he led her back to the table. He sat down beside her, and they started to talk as if they'd never left off.

Almost at the end of the evening there was a cabaret; six slim young girls, their bodies coated with suntan lotion, danced round the room whilst a young man trailed a microphone and sang how he'd left his heart somewhere or other.

Mary felt relaxed and happy, and it was then that Stephen reached out for her hand.

Surprise and a slight sense of shock held her still for a moment, then as the pressure of his fingers increased, she returned it. As his fingers gently traced the veins on the inside of her wrist she felt her very bones liquefy with a feeling of tenderness and an indefinable longing.

Then it was all over – time for the last waltz. Robert, flushed and more than a little unsteady on his feet, claimed her dutifully to propel her backwards round the room.

She said a courteous goodnight to Stephen. All the way home in the car, she sat in her corner, reliving the feel of his hand on hers, and later, in her bed next to Robert's, she lay awake listening to his rhythmic snoring, wishing for a soothing sleep that wouldn't come.

She hadn't been able to believe it when he'd rung her this morning, for though he had been in her mind constantly, his had been the last voice in the world she'd expected to hear.

He wanted to see her again . . . She would go, and they'd talk and she'd tell him all the little things that normally she would never have thought worth mentioning. He'd listen with the grave way he had, nodding every now and again as if what she was saying was vitally interesting.

There would be no harm in it, no harm at all, because as anyone knew, a man and a woman could lunch together because they were friends, and they liked each other's company. And that was all there was to it . . .

The telephone rang. She went to answer it, and carefully wrote down her mother-in-law's Friday shopping list. Then she went upstairs to get ready for her walk.

Later, when she was ready to go out, as she pulled on her gloves in the hall, she remembered again the touch of his fingers on her wrist, and for a moment the heady feeling of joy, the melting sense of longing, overwhelmed her again.

She had always prided herself on being an honest person, and she would be honest with herself now . . .

When she met Stephen, she wouldn't be meeting him as a friend. She would be meeting him because she was already more than a little way to falling in love with

71

him. He was a lonely man, a man of integrity, as Robert had said, and telephoning her this morning hadn't been an easy thing for him to do.

She knew that he didn't look upon her simply as an easy conquest. He had liked her, he'd responded to something in her, some warmth, some sympathy that she, from the depth of her own lonely heart, had been only too ready to give.

Mary sat down on the little chair by the small table. They would meet the next week, but it wouldn't end there, she knew that. They would meet again, perhaps round at his flat, and he would make love to her, and she would let him, because from just the touch of his hand on her wrist, she had known how it would be.

And because she was as she was, she would be committed. There would be no turning back then. Her thoughts raced ahead.

She would tell Robert, and the children would have to know, and what had started off as an innocently loving friendship would end for both of them in sordid disillusionment.

Peeling off her gloves, Mary stared at the telephone . . .

Her marriage to Robert was sound, no different, she was sure, from the marriages of countless other couples. He was ambitious; he had risen to the position he held because of his hard work, seeing to it that she had a lovely home, and that the children had had the best education his money could give them.

Perhaps in his own way he loved her; perhaps, now that she knew she could attract another man, it would give her the confidence and the poise that Robert had always wanted to see in her.

Picking up the telephone she started to dial.

She was doing the right thing. All that was in her told her that she was doing the right thing, but, 'Oh

Stephen,' she whispered before he answered, 'I could have loved you. I could have loved you so much, so very much.'

What was it he'd said? *It's easy to be brave when we care enough.*

But in that he'd been wrong. It wasn't easy at all.

Please, Please, Noel

All the way home, Beth's mind seethed with the injustice of it all . . .

She knew she was plump and tall, a good head taller than the rest of the thirteen-year-olds in her form at school. She recognised that. She was big and fat, and her shoes were a shame-making size seven.

She had set her heart on playing Noah in the end-of-term play. She knew she would have made a marvellous Noah, with a grey beard stuck on her chin, and she would have strutted round the stage, and called on God to deliver them from the flood, but instead of that the part had gone to Margot Baines, who went to elocution lessons, and fancied herself no end.

Beth was to be an elephant, one of a pair of elephants, with a papier-mâché head stuck on her shoulders, and a grey trunk stuffed with cotton wool to wave in triumph as she climbed up into the Ark.

Typecast, with no regard at all for her finer feelings, no taking into account that the boys from the Grammar School would be invited *en bloc* to watch the final dress rehearsal.

The avenue where she lived terminated at the Green Belt, and a biting east wind blew from the open fields, stinging her pale cheeks and making her eyes water, but she walked on, head bent, her whole mind intent on reaching home to pour out the whole sorry tale to her mother.

But as she let herself in with her key, dropping her books on the hall table – to carry a case or satchel that particular year was not in fashion – she heard her mother's voice speaking on the telephone extension in her room upstairs.

Slowly, Beth climbed the carpeted stairs, one hand trailing the banister, and it wasn't until she reached the top that what her mother was saying made any conscious impression.

'You can't say that, darling,' her mother was saying, and her voice was not the warm, comforting voice that Beth knew, but that of a child, crying out in hurt bewilderment. 'I've *got* to see you again. You couldn't be that cruel. Not after . . . after everything.'

Beth stood quite still, totally unable to move.

'Even if she knows,' her mother was saying, 'and she is only guessing, we can be more careful.' There was a small silence. 'Please, Noel. Please, please, don't say goodbye like this. Not on the telephone. Yes, I know I've no pride, I never did have where you're concerned, but I can't help it, and I can't . . . you *can't*, Noel!'

The name seemed to be torn from her and, with a wildly beating heart, Beth turned round and crept quietly downstairs, and stood in the hall, staring at the stricken face reflected in the hall mirrors.

From upstairs she heard the click of the receiver being replaced, and with an understanding far beyond comprehension and almost without volition, she opened and closed the heavy front door with a bang, and called upstairs: 'Mummy! It's me!'

And after a barely imperceptible pause, her mother's voice spiralled downstairs.

'Coming, lovey. Just a minute. I'll be down in a minute.'

In the kitchen, warm and blessedly normal, Beth stood by the dresser, her usual dive into the pantry for the biscuit tin forgotten.

Her mother, her ordinary, kind, far from beautiful mother, had a *lover*. A man called Noel who didn't want her any more.

Beth unfastened her white raincoat, worn, contrary to school regulations, slid it off and draped it over a chair. She had read enough, seen enough plays on television, to have understood the implication in a flash.

But that kind of thing happened to other people, other mothers, actresses with slim figures and dark anguish-filled eyes. Not to mothers who wore tweed skirts and unglamorous sweaters, who made scones for tea, and went to church on Sundays.

Hearing soft footsteps in the hall, she opened the pantry door and stuck her head inside. She couldn't meet her mother's eyes. Not yet. She grabbed the square biscuit tin and pretended to be engrossed in prising off the lid.

'Had a good day, lovey?' her mother said from behind her and, if Beth hadn't heard the telephone conversation just three short minutes before, she would never have been able to detect the slight wobble in her voice.

'Horrible,' she said, emerging with two unwanted biscuits. 'Foul and horrible.'

And now she could see that her mother had been crying, and her cheeks were flushed and, instead of wanting to know immediately the cause of the foulness and horribleness, she walked over to the sink and busied herself with filling the kettle.

Only after she had set it on the gas stove and got out two cups and saucers from the hanging cupboard, did she speak again:

'Aren't you going to tell me what went wrong?'

And now she smiled, and the smile was no more than the lifting of the corners of her mouth. Her eyes looked dead, and Beth took a bite of a biscuit without knowing what she was doing, and choked on it.

'I'm to be an elephant in the end-of-term play,' she made herself say, 'and I wanted to be Noah, and I've to wear a foul grey tunic thing, and we've to make it,

77

and Miss horrible Graham is borrowing heads for all the animals to wear from a theatrical agency, and mine will have a trunk. A horrible long thing to wave about.'

Normally, her mother would have known immediately the reason for her wounded pride. She was always telling Beth how lucky she was to be so tall; how some day when she could wear smart clothes she would be *glad* she was tall, and that small feet would look silly on a tall girl.

All the things Beth didn't believe yet still wanted to hear. But now her mother merely brushed her hair away from her forehead with a weary gesture, and told Beth not to speak with her mouth full.

'I don't want a cup of tea,' Beth said. 'I'm going upstairs to do my homework.'

And she walked out of the kitchen, collecting her books from the hall table, and rushing upstairs two steps at a time.

Her mother wouldn't follow her. Beth doubted whether she'd even heard her properly, and in her bedroom she threw herself flat on her bed, and stared unseeing at the ceiling.

All the way home she had comforted herself with the knowledge of how it would be. Her mother would listen sympathetically and, more like two friends than mother and daughter, they would sit together round the kitchen table, sipping tea, and when all the tale was told her mother would say, as she always said when something really unspeakably dreadful had happened: 'Now please don't take on so, lovey. In a hundred years from now, it will all be the same. Just you wait and see.'

And at the familiar, not very funny joke, Beth would have to smile, and her mother would come and put her arm round her shoulders as she sat there at the table, and she would lean against her, and smell the warm mother smell of her, and miraculously everything would be all right again.

Beth closed her eyes and heard her mother's voice again. *Please, Noel, please, please . . .*

And she was old enough and sensitive enough to recognize heart-break when she heard it speaking.

She lay there for a full half hour, in the languid laziness of adolescence, issues too great for her to comprehend clouding her mind. Her mother and another man. Did they . . . ?

She tried to imagine her ordinary, comfortable little mother – Beth had inherited her size from her father's side of the family – held in another man's arms, and the image excited, disturbed and repelled her at one and the same time.

The room grew dark, and winter rain lashed the window, but she didn't move to switch on the light, or get up to draw the curtains. She wondered what her father would do if he found out? Would he go and fight the other man, the mysterious Noel?

But she couldn't imagine her father fighting anyone.

A tall, well-built man, he came and went from the house, wearing a briefcase like a second skin, and every evening after supper he would work on his 'papers' in the dining-room, emerging around nine o'clock to sprawl exhausted in his chair, to watch television with his eyes closed.

They didn't quarrel. There were no dramatic shouting rows to justify her mother's behaviour. But then they didn't talk much either.

Sighing, Beth raised one arm to switch on the overhead light, then shaded her eyes from the sudden glare.

She had never examined her parents' relationship before, not in this way. But then, she had never needed to. It was enough that they were there, dependable, safe, her mother and her father, a family unit. Sitting up, she reached to the foot of the bed for her biology exercise book, and started an uninspired drawing of a rabbit's alimentary canal. When her father came home she would tell *him* about the school play, and get him to see that she could not be expected to suffer the indignity of it all.

But, sitting opposite him at the table, and watching the way he ate his food silently, almost as if he had no idea of what he was eating, she knew that she could never talk to him about it.

He wouldn't see why the part was an offence to her pride; he would merely nod now and again, and tell her not to worry, and dismiss it at that, as though telling her not to worry solved everything.

That was the way he was, and glancing at her mother, eyes lowered to her plate obviously willing herself to chew, then swallow, Beth wondered if *that* was why . . . ?

Had this man, this Noel, listened to her mother talking to him? Really listened with all his mind, not with part of it on the papers in his ever-ready briefcase?

'Had a good day?' her mother was saying, and 'Much as usual,' her father said, and her voice was dead like her eyes, and he didn't notice a thing.

The tight feeling in Beth's over-developed chest rose up to her throat, and threatened her eyes with the prick of tears.

'This is good,' she said desperately. 'Shepherd's pie is my favourite, don't you like shepherd's pie, Daddy?'

And he smiled and said, 'I like everything your mother cooks, she knows that,' and for a wild moment Beth hated him.

Then she remembered it was her mother she should be hating, and she refused a second helping, saying that she wasn't all that hungry, and after supper she went straight back upstairs to finish her homework.

Later they sat together round the television set, her mother in her corner, with the table lamp switched on, and knitting as though everything was just the same. As if she had never pleaded with another man on the telephone, begging him to see her again, just once more. . . .

And in his own chair her father dozed, his long legs stretched out in front of him, and on the screen, a little round man made jokes that nobody laughed at, whilst outside the rain lashed the window.

At ten o'clock, just before Beth went up to bed, the telephone rang, and at a nod from her father she went to answer it. Her mother's knitting needles were still, and her eyes held a look, half fear, half hope. But it was only a man from the Works, and after a long discussion her father popped his head round the door, said something important had cropped up and that he would have to work on his papers again.

And Beth left her mother sitting there, with the knitting rolled up now, her hands idle in her tweed-skirted lap, thinking about *him*. She knew that for sure.

Just on impulse she went into the dining-room where her father was already spreading the papers out on the dining-room table. Shyly, because she knew he was a man who shied away from anything he described as 'soppy', she bent and kissed the top of his head, right in the middle of the tiny thinning patch of hair.

'What's that in aid of?' he said without looking up, but he was smiling, and she went upstairs, tired out with the emotion of it all, and fell asleep almost immediately, and dreamed she was leading a herd of elephants along the high street, whilst all the boys from the Youth Club stood on the pavement, jeering.

They were big elephants, huge, fat, with their grey tails entwined round the trunks of the one behind, and she was the biggest of them all. . . .

She woke up with a start, and when she saw by the luminous dial on her bedside clock that the time was three o'clock, she couldn't believe it. She never woke in the middle of the night, never, and sometimes she had to be shaken awake by her mother when the time came to get up.

She could hear the faint sounds of someone moving about on the landing, and she listened, holding her breath, to the soft sound of footsteps going downstairs. Then she heard the careful opening and closing of the kitchen door, and was instantly wide awake.

It only took her a minute to make up her mind. Then, groping for her dressing-gown, afraid to put on her light, she crept downstairs, along the hall, and found her mother sitting at the kitchen table, her hands clasped together on its red Formica top, just sitting there, immobile, staring into space, with that awful dead expression in her eyes.

At the sight of Beth she gripped the edges of the table hard.

'What's the matter, lovey?' Her voice was lifeless, but she made an attempt at a smile. 'Can't you sleep either? It must be the wind. More like March than January. I was just going to make a cup of tea. Would you like one?'

'I've got a pain,' Beth lied, making a vague circle in the direction of her middle. 'You sit there, Mummy, I'll make the tea.'

She had to turn away. She couldn't bear to see the look of utter and hopeless anguish in her mother's eyes, so she busied herself with the kettle and setting out cups.

'We won't bother with saucers,' she said, and her mother said something she couldn't catch, and her voice sounded again like it had on the telephone, like a child's voice crying in the dark.

Suddenly Beth knew should couldn't bear it any longer. She didn't understand. Perhaps she would never understand, but she loved her mother with a love that had no need of understanding, and she loved her father too, lying asleep upstairs, tired out with work and oblivious to it all.

Going over to the table she pulled her mother to her feet and enfolded her in her arms, and it didn't strike her as being in the least incongruous that she was six inches taller, and that her mother's head could quite easily rest on her shoulder.

'Don't be sad, Mummy,' she said. 'Don't take on so. In a hundred years from now, it will all be the same. Just you wait and see.'

If Only We Could Lock Up Linda

Our daughter's name is Linda. She is sixteen years old, and when she told us that she had decided she would go away with us to Italy, we were more than pleased; we were delighted.

Even though her attitude was one of doing us a big favour, we were both touched and overjoyed.

'I'm quite sure there wouldn't have been any problem in leaving her at home,' my wife said, 'but you do hear of such peculiar things happening when parents go away.'

'I know,' I said, thinking of drug parties in general and Stevie Shaw in particular.

Stevie Shaw was Linda's boyfriend. He had shoulder-length hair, a droopy moustache and a beard, but we had told ourselves that appearances mattered not a single jot, even when he called for her wearing jeans so moulded to his legs as to be almost obscene and wool tops that had surely shrunk in the wash.

My wife told me that what bit she could see of his face was quite nice but, all the same, most nights we lay uneasy in our beds waiting for the sound of his souped-up car turning into the gravel drive.

He drove it as if he were on the last lap of the Monte Carlo Rally and there was never any sleep for us until we heard Linda's footsteps on the stairs. We used to wait up for her but, when we grew thin and pale from lack of sleep, we told our daughter that we *trusted* her, after all.

She was the only girl in Middlesex who had to be in by midnight, she told us sorrowfully and, when I reminded her it was eleven o'clock on weekdays, she raised her blue eyes ceilingwards, as if to pray for patience to tide her over to my next remark.

So life went on and Stevie Shaw seemed to have moved in with us. I became used to bumping into him in the hall, hairy and furtive, and noted that he treated me with a kind of unspoken contempt.

My wife and I started casting hopeful glances at the boy across the street who belonged to the Young Conservatives, and sometimes wore a very smart suit.

We told ourselves Stevie Shaw was just a 'phase', and looked ahead to the two weeks in Italy, and prayed that, in our daughter's case, absence from the loved one would not make her heart grow fonder.

And so the holiday came round, and at the airport, Stevie Shaw said a fond farewell to our Linda, holding her to his droopy moustache. It was raining, and he was wearing a tartan blanket as an overcoat and we pretended not to know either of them.

It was still raining when we arrived at our hotel in Italy, but we were perfectly happy, because Linda talked to us as if we might possibly be human, and we went to bed early, promising ourselves, my wife and I, that we would forget the existence of Stevie Shaw for the next fourteen days and concentrate on our holiday.

The next day the sun shone, and on the beach we staked our claim to three lounging chairs, plus one fringed umbrella for me to lurk under, because I am suspicious of too much sun.

Linda looked young and touchingly innocent in her scarlet swimsuit and we watched with pride as she coated every inch of her slim body with suntan lotion and scorning the chair, lay back on a striped towel, awaiting results.

The Italian boy in charge of our little slice of beach was tall, with hair that brushed his shoulders, a droopy moustache, and a gold band encircling his left ankle.

I positioned my umbrella in deference to the chang-
ing rays of the sun, and my wife turned over to toast
the backs of her legs. A peace I had not known for a
long time enveloped my whole being, and I could not
believe my ears when, over our spaghetti at lunch,
Linda told us that she was going out with the beach
boy that evening.

'But you don't know him!' I said, and she sighed at
me.

Apparently some of my views were absolutely
pathetic. And old-fashioned. As well as naïve. My wife
stopped twirling her spaghetti round her fork in gay
holiday style, her appetite quite gone.

'But does he speak English?'

Linda shook her head.

'And you can't speak a word of Italian. How will
you even communicate with each other, dear?'

'We'll manage,' our daughter reassured us, and her
meaning seemed to be charged with undertones. Sinis-
ter ones at that.

My wife told me that what bit she had seen of his
face seemed to be quite nice, and I told her that our
Linda had her head screwed on all right, and that she
knew we *trusted* her, after all.

The trouble was, did the Italian beach boy know that
we trusted *him*? And I became used to bumping into
him in the marble-floored foyer, hairy and furtive, and
noted that he treated me with a kind of unspoken and
foreign contempt.

And so there we were, my wife and I, night after
night, lying uneasy in our beds, listening for the sound
of Linda's returning footsteps in the corridor outside,
knowing that we would never sleep until we knew she
was safe and sound, asleep in her own little room.

The beach boy had an old souped-up car, which he
drove as if it were on the last lap of the Monte Carlo

Rally and, when he wasn't busy sweeping the beach, they were completely inseparable.

Stevie Shaw was waiting for us at the airport on our return home, but Linda could hardly be bothered to exchange a word with him. Her heart, it was obvious, she had left behind under an Italian sky.

Somehow Stevie Shaw didn't look quite so hairy, quite so unkempt, and when the moustache drooped disconsolately at our daughter's treatment of him, I even found it in my heart to feel sorry for him.

So did my wife.

'You know, I always said he had a nice face,' she said. . . .

Different from the Rest

I am an intensely practical person. I have to be because everyone else in my family is quite dotty.

We live in a crumbling ruin of a house, and my mother paints. Not the woodwork, unfortunately, but massive poster-like pictures, and when she's not painting, she sculpts. Ugly brown vases, that even a stone-age man wouldn't have given cave-room to, and chalk-white heads that leer at us with sightless eyes from the kitchen dresser, and even more unlikely places.

My sixteen-year-old brother, Lancelot, is at ballet school, and spends his time around the house doing one of two things. Either practising Nijinsky-like leaps, or lying flat on the floor reading poetry.

My father writes. Not science-fiction or spy stories, but romantic novels, tender, beautiful, heart-stopping tales of love, under the pen-name of Coralyn Silver, and endearingly funny stories for children, about an Australian worm called Wumba-tumba.

Even our cat has an artistic temperament, rubbing itself against our legs one minute in sickening devotion, then stalking majestically past us the next. He answers, when he feels like it, to the name of Heathfield.

So you see how essential it is in a family like mine, for one person to have their feet, not only firmly on the ground, but a couple of inches underneath.

At school I was good at maths, absolutely flabber-gasting my mother, who has never really grasped the fact that two and two make four.

So I took a secretarial course, and landed myself a well-paid job with a firm of accountants.

'How can you?' said Mother, the day I came home

triumphant from the interview. 'All those figures and dry-as-dust phraseology. Positively soul-destroying, I call it.'

My father took his hands off the typewriter keys for a moment, and rubbed them together with glee. 'Now you'll be able to do my income tax returns, beastly depressing things that they are.' Then he went back to another exciting episode in the life of Wumba-tumba, and forgot that I was there.

So that was how I took over the balancing of the household budget; no mean task when my father's cheques come in mostly at a sluggish dribble, and my mother sells a painting every six months or so. But I worked at it until we were sure of at least one square meal a day, and in between I met James.

James was newly, but fully chartered in my firm as an accountant, with a tidy, accurate mind, and a tidy, accurate way of kissing me.

He was everything my family was not – methodical, practical, and when he proposed I accepted him with humble thankfulness.

With James I would live in a house where the outside was painted once every two years, and where meals arrived on time, and where we didn't need to hide in the pantry when the milkman called for the week's money.

He wasn't a bit like the hero in one of my father's novels. He was square and solid, and wore his hair cut short back and sides. But he was kind, and thoughtful, and intensely practical. Like me . . .

The first time I took him home for a meal, my family made an all-out effort, which touched me immensely, but left James, I could see, rather perplexed.

Mother took off her smock and appeared in a paisley-patterned dress, with a cross-over fluted effect, and

Father came out of his study, and made what he thought was man-to-man conversation with James.

As he'd been closeted with Wumba-tumba all day, it wasn't too successful, but I left them drinking beer together, and escaped to the kitchen, where Mother was putting the finishing touches to her idea of a good conventional meal.

Lance came home from his day's stint at ballet school, looking pale and tired, as though he'd been grown in the dark. I took over from mother, who was frantically sieving the lumps out of the gravy.

But everything was all right.

James behaved beautifully, and told my parents all about EFTA, and the Common Market. They listened as if he were bringing news from outer space, and when Mother apologised for the lemon mousse, which we had to drink instead of eat, James smiled indulgently, and said that he liked his mousse that way.

I thought he looked a bit shattered when he came out of the bathroom later, and when I went in myself, I saw the reason why.

Reposing on top of the lavatory cistern were two well-formed ears belonging to Mother's latest creation (a bust of Molière) and on the linen box, an erotic sketch she'd done of Father in the nude.

James and I went for a walk on the heath, and it was a blustery evening, all shifting clouds. Tall trees tossing their branches at us, and James being, I thought, rather silent.

'You're very different from the rest of your family, aren't you?' he said carefully. 'I mean, you're not *creative* in any way.'

'Not in any way,' I said firmly, but added loyally: 'They're very sweet, you know, and clever, and immensely talented.'

'Oh, very sweet,' said James, in what I suspected

was a slightly patronising tone. 'Creative types usually are.'

I could have hit him, but instead I allowed him to pull me close into his arms, and when he kissed me, I responded dutifully, and told myself that this was where I really belonged. Safe in James's arms, held close against the hardness of his chest, and listening to him telling me about the house we would have when we were married. . . .

A bungalow it was to be, with a garden for James to potter in, and a kitchen for me, streamlined and efficient, like an ad in an American house magazine.

I lay in bed that night thinking about James pottering, and me turning out delicious little dinners in my streamlined kitchen, and I found that I had a headache coming on, and went into the bathroom for the aspirin bottle.

It wasn't in the medicine chest, of course. I was silly looking for it there in the first place, and I went downstairs and found it on top of the bureau, next to Lance's Tennyson, and a tube of Mother's paint.

Heathfield rubbed himself against my legs, and I took him back to bed with me, and he lay curled up against my feet, all breathing fur and cosy comfort.

James was away on business for the whole of the next week. Tunbridge Wells, I think it was, and I stayed at home and was faithful to him, washing my hair, and watching the ancient television in the downstairs cloakroom. We keep it there because my father says it is death to inspiration, and I feel I should have put that in capital letters because he says it so often.

He was taking my mother to the theatre one evening that week. Not to a theatre in town, but to a community theatre, about an hour's drive away, where the actors wear no make-up, and spurn the use of scenery, merely coming out into the middle of the stage, saying their pieces, then walking off, taking the scenery with them if it isn't needed for the next bit.

At the last minute Father decided he couldn't go, being involved in what he described as a purple passage in chapter seven.

'Vanda is on the point of succumbing, and if I break off now, she may never work herself up into the mood again,' he told me seriously. 'She's rather a prude, I'm afraid. You go with your mother, there's a good girl. It'll all be over by the time you get back.'

And so I went, partly because I didn't want to see Mother disappointed, and partly because she drives the car as though she's on the last lap of the Monte Carlo Rally, and it won't stand up to that kind of treatment, being vintage 1949.

We turned back twice, once because she'd forgotten the tickets, and again for her spectacles.

Actually they were in her handbag all the time, but she couldn't 'see' them there. 'Next to that pile of unpaid bills,' she told me, smiling, and I couldn't be cross, because when Mother smiles it is impossible to be cross.

She was wearing a tartan cloak over her best twin-set and pearls, and a feather that was supposed to pass for a hat, pinned to her soft, curly hair.

'It's lovely to dress up once in a while,' she told me, as I turned the car for the third time out of the drive, and I smiled back at her, loving her, and thinking how deliciously dotty she was.

'I love you,' I wanted to say, but I didn't because people with their feet on the ground don't talk like that. Not practical, sensible people like me.

We were late, of course, and we got glares from the third row of the audience when we pushed passed them, treading on their toes to find our seats.

'What a gorgeous young man,' Mother whispered, and was instantly hushed into silence by a whiskery type in the row behind.

But he *was* gorgeous, the young man on the stage. There was no doubt at all about that.

He was speaking his lines in a voice all melted butter and honey, with the faintest of Welsh accents, and he was tall, dark-haired, a bit too thin perhaps, with worry lines on his lean face.

I listened to him in spellbound admiration; to the way he captivated the audience, the way he stood alone out there on the stage, with just a little hard chair for company.

After he'd gone off carrying the little hard chair underneath one arm, a small woman with a magnificent bust came on, and told us that she was Mother Earth.

'She might be now,' said Mother, in a hoarse whisper, 'but when I knew her, she was Tilly Garden.'

'Tilly Garden?' I hissed back.

Mother nodded. 'Playing Hamlet in the end-of-term play.'

My eyebrows must have expressed acute surprise, and Mother's voice was haughty. 'She was magnificent!' she said.

Immediately the performance was over she insisted on going round the back, and greeting her old school friend.

'It must be all of thirty years since we met,' she said, her cape swinging out in excited folds as we pushed open a door marked 'Private, Players Only'.

In spite of the thirty years, they fell on each other's necks, each swearing that the other hadn't changed one bit.

I left them giggling together and wandered away down a dark brown corridor towards the welcome sound of rattling tea cups.

The young man who had spoken his lines so beautifully was leaning against a wooden draining-board, sipping a cup of tea. He smiled when he saw me, and pointed to a big aluminium teapot.

'There's a cup left if you squeeze it hard enough. Here, I'll do it for you,' he said.

As he poured me a cup of tea, stewed thick and half cold, I saw that his eyes were a dark grey, not flinty and hard, but the colour of Heathfield's soft coat. They were dreaming eyes, like those of a young child.

'Don't you want to know who I am and what I'm doing here?' I asked him at last.

The grey eyes twinkled down at me. 'I don't care who you are. You're nice, that much is obvious.'

I tried to look dignified. 'I'm Becky Lee, and my mother's out there talking to Mother Earth. They were at school together, but then she was Hamlet. I hope I make myself clear?'

He held out his free hand, and we shook solemnly. 'And I'm Gareth Hughes, and the others have gone on to a party. You must come with me, your mother can follow on with – *who* did you say?'

'Tilly Garden,' I explained, 'but that would be her maiden name, and I can't come to the party. My mother will want to get back to my father – they're funny like that. Next year is their silver wedding, and apart from the war, they've never spent a single night away from each other.

I remember how James had smiled when I'd told him that, but Gareth nodded, as though it was the most natural statement.

'They're coming now,' he said, as two sets of high-pitched giggles approached along the dark brown corridor. 'We'll see what a little persuasion can do.'

And the grey eyes worked the same magic on Mother as they'd worked on me. Gareth found her a telephone box, and she rang Father, and in twenty minutes flat we found ourselves in an untidy bed-sitting-room at the top of a tall Victorian house, drinking sherry out of tooth mugs, and sitting on a single bed, along with ten or more other people.

There were books everywhere, and a pair of silver shoes on the mantelpiece, and someone in a corner was reciting a John Betjeman poem aloud. Mother had discarded the cape, and was telling intimate details of our family life to a bull-like man with a black Father Christmas beard, and Tilly Garden was sitting on the floor, her long necklace in her hand, and her eyes tight shut, apparently telling her beads.

They were all deliciously dotty, and I relaxed. It was, I realised wryly, a kind of home from home.

Gareth was sitting right beside me, so close that if I turned my head to speak to him, we were only a kiss away. His mouth was long and sensitive, and when he smiled I could see a tiny white filling in his front tooth, and all the time the grey eyes were watching me.

'I want to know everything about you, Becky,' he said, 'so begin.'

There wasn't much to tell, but he listened intently, nodding every now and again, as though what I was saying was the most important thing in the whole world.

When I told him about my job as secretary to an accountant, and how I was studying for my own accountancy examinations, he shook his dark head.

'A soul-destroying occupation for a lovely girl like you,' he said, almost exactly as Mother had said.

'And you?' I asked, and he told me that he was staying with the company for a full season, then hoping to get into rep.

'Anywhere, I don't mind,' he said. 'It's experience I'm after, and although the pay is poor, I'll be doing what I was born to do, and that's the main thing.'

I sighed. It was the same old record being played all over again.

'What is money, anyway?' he asked me, just as my own father had asked me so many, many times.

'Some day I'll be discovered,' he told me seriously, the grey eyes aglow. 'Shakespeare is my real love,' and he started to quote a long speech from *Romeo and Juliet*. The others sharing the bed fell silent, and we listened to the deep, wonderful Welsh voice reciting the beautiful words.

But I knew that he was saying them to me alone.

'Come with me,' he said, somewhere around midnight. 'I've something to show you.'

So I followed him out of the crowded room, across a narrow landing, and out through a door to the fire-escape.

It was a cool night, a night without stars, and his arm was lightly round my shoulders, and I could see his profile and the shape of his hawk-like nose, and the way his hair grew long and to an endearing peak in the nape of his neck.

'All those people out there,' he said, 'asleep in their houses; asleep and missing so much. And in the morning, getting up and going out to their safe little jobs. Waiting in the station for the eight-fifteen into town, then sitting at their desks, opening their dry-as-dust ledgers, working away at the figures that seem so important. Then coming home on the five-fifteen, to where their wives wait with a sherry, and a vitamin-filled casserole in the oven.' He grinned.

'Not for me,' he said.

I moved away from him, and leaned my bare arms on the rusty iron railing. 'Some people are happy that way,' I said firmly.

People like James, I thought.

'Me, for instance,' I said out loud. 'What's wrong in

solidity and punctuality, and in knowing where the next meal's coming from? Tell me that!'

To my dismay, my voice trembled, and when he came behind me, and I felt the strength of his arms around me, I leaned against him in inexplicable relief.

'And not for you, either, Becky, my love,' the dark brown voice said in my ear, and gently he turned me round, and traced with his finger the outline of my mouth before he kissed me.

And oh, it was a tender kiss, not a bit like the tidy, accurate ones I got from James, and I slid my arms round his neck and kissed him back.

'You're my sort of girl,' he said. 'I knew it the first moment I saw you, and I'm falling in love with you, and because you are my sort of girl, you believe me. I'm right, aren't I, Becky?'

'You're right,' I said, 'and how can I not believe you, when my own parents met and married within a month, to love each other for ever and ever amen?'

'A month's a long time,' said Gareth Hughes. 'What I really had in mind was next week.'

And I laughed out loud as he swung me up until my feet were clear off the ground.

Where they belonged. I knew that now.

Plain Jane

When they told twelve-year-old Jane that she had to have a tonsilectomy, she didn't mind in the least. Intelligent, and bent at the moment on becoming a veterinary surgeon, she merely pushed her horn-rimmed spectacles further up the bridge of her small nose.

'Will I be able to bring them home, and pickle them in a jar?'

Her father lowered his newspaper just a fraction of an inch. 'That's a good idea, poppet. We could put them on the mantelpiece, and show them off to visitors.'

Her mother shuddered. 'Once the nasty things have gone, we never want to think about them again. They've caused quite enough trouble as it is.'

Jane exchanged a conspiratorial wink with her father before he silently disappeared behind his rather tattered newspaper again . . .

Now that it was all settled she could hardly wait to tell the girls at school about it. The youngest in her form by almost a year, she worried constantly about what she thought was her unpopularity. Constantly, it seemed, she was left alone, an envious onlooker on the fringe of things. She put it all down to her lack of 'glamour', and meaningless phrases like puppy plumpness did nothing to mollify. Why couldn't they just admit that she was big and fat, and leave it at that?

So, during the long hour or so before she fell asleep, she decided that it would have to be far more startling than a tonsilectomy if she were to make any impression on the girls in her form.

An amputation? No, the fact that she would still have the requisite number of limbs when she returned from hospital would be hard to explain away. It would have to be something obscure and internal. Feverishly her mind ranged over the parts of the anatomy her one term of biology had encompassed, and she came to the conclusion that an inflamed appendix was perhaps the safest story to keep to.

She saw herself lying on the asphalt netball court, having shot the winning goal. One hand clasped to her side, she gasped through ashen lips that it was nothing. Just a pain she'd had all through the game. The girls gathered round her as an ambulance pulled up with a loud screech of brakes, and two strong men carried her out to it, on a stretcher, wrapped in a big red blanket.

'Hospital blankets are red so that the blood doesn't show,' she said aloud, startling her mother, who was at that moment tiptoeing into the room to close the window.

'She's *dwelling* on it,' she heard her tell her father.

Jane pulled the sheet over her head, and back at school, after an operation necessitating at least fifty stitches, received the netball cup from a headmistress, moved beyond words. After that so many girls wanted to walk with her round the playing field at breaks, they had to draw lots for the honour.

As soon as she arrived at school the next morning, she dived down the steps into the basement cloakroom where Aileen Mair, a tall sophisticated thirteen-year-old, was holding her customary morning court.

Aileen was at the mirror, combing her fringe into fashionable spiky points, surrounded by a circle of admirers, and normally Jane would have hung up her hat and blazer, aloof, isolated, and shelled around in her normal solitude.

But today she changed hurriedly into her indoor shoes and, heedless of the sudden changing of the assembly bell, she stepped forward, her heart thudding loudly in her disappointingly flat chest.

100

'You know that I was away from school yesterday?' she began hopefully.

Aileen raised her eyebrows that she plucked regularly under the cover of her desk-lid, and Jane rushed on, the words tumbling over themselves.

'Well, I went to see a specialist – a Harley Street specialist,' she improvised. 'And I have to have a serious operation, or I may die.'

Aileen exchanged a glance with Pamela Woods who wore eye-shadow on the way home from school, and wrote notes to a boy at the County Grammar School.

'An appendix,' Jane said in desperation as they moved towards the wide oak staircase, 'an appendix that is ready to burst at any minute.'

'No talking in the corridors,' said a prefect, standing in smug splendour at the head of the stairs, and Aileen, who regarded all prefects as beneath her contempt, said out of the side of her mouth, 'There's nothing to having an appendix out. I had mine out when I was six.'

And during the singing of the first hymn Jane saw Aileen and Pamela watching her, helpless with giggles.

She had only made things worse. As usual they were laughing at her. Longingly she stared at the long neck of Margaret Alton, the girl in front of her. Margaret had been drawn into Aileen's charmed circle solely on account of having a brother who looked just like Scott Walker.

Jane bowed her head low during the prayer for the day, and prayed a private and anxious little prayer: 'Make me beautiful, so that I can have a boyfriend, and if you could arrange for one of the boys from the Priory School to pass me a note when they come for musical appreciation today, I'd be most grateful. Amen.'

Most of the girls in her form had a boyfriend. Even

Malcolm Greenhill, who smoked at the bus stop and had spots all over his face, was sighed over by Margaret Alton. The whole thing was very puzzling to Jane.

What was there about boys that was so special, after all? She didn't love any of them. To her they were noisy, rough and rude, and it was quite apparent that none of them loved *her*.

Would she have to grow up unloved and unloving to the end of her days?

She tried to talk to her mother about it that same evening. 'Aileen Mair is in love with the head boy from the Priory School. He took her to the cinema, and he kissed her,' she said casually as they cleared the table after their supper.

Her mother bit her lips into a thin line, and looked angry, and when Jane carried the plates through into the kitchen she heard her voice through the open service-hatch.

'I thought Jane would have been safe from that kind of thing for a while yet. Girls are growing up far too quickly these days.'

Thoughtfully Jane gathered the coffee cups together. Why was it unsafe to love someone? Her parents loved each other, she knew. What had she said to upset her mother so much?

The sudden ringing of the telephone made her jump and almost drop the lid of the coffee pot. She heard her mother hurry into the hall, and tried to eavesdrop on the conversation.

'That was the hospital, darling,' her mother told her brightly. 'A little girl admitted today has developed a temperature, so they've sent her home, and Sister says if we take you along in the morning you can have her bed. Isn't that splendid?'

Jane agreed that indeed it was, and saw the girls at school wondering if perhaps, after all, there had been some truth in what she'd said, and feeling sorry. Opening the service-hatch she passed on the news to her father.

'A bit of a sore throat for a day or two, lovey, that's all it means,' he said, and Jane had a sudden urge to go and sit on his knee and pat his face, like she used to do when she was young. Her father had always told her the truth about things, no matter what, and if he said that was all it would be, then she believed him.

The next morning Jane undressed by a bed, enclosed in a screen of rose-printed cretonne. She had been allocated a bed in women's surgical because the children's ward was full, and her mother, waving cheerfully, left her sitting up, her hands folded self-consciously on to the neatly turned-down sheet.

Shyly, Jane stared round her.

On her left, a lady with white hair and a face to match was propped against a mound of pillows. Her eyes were closed; she was so still that Jane wondered if she could have died without anyone noticing, and was immeasurably relieved to see her take a paper tissue from a box on her locker, and touch it to the end of her nose.

Jane turned her head away, and looked directly into the eyes of the girl on her right.

She was quite old, about twenty-five, Jane guessed, and pinkly plump in the quilted bed-jacket. Her hair was pale mouse, pulled back from her shiny forehead with a rubber-band. Freckles as big as moles stood out on her white skin, and when she smiled at her she showed what seemed to be more than the usual number of large cream teeth.

'You're in for tonsils, aren't you?' she said.

Jane nodded. 'They're septic,' she said proudly.

The dinner was being wheeled in, but she wasn't allowed any, and she saw with surprise that the pale lady sat up and ate two large helpings of everything, finishing off with a cup of strong tea, and a minty sweet from her locker.

The toothy girl was helped out of bed, and wheeled away by a physiotherapist, and when she'd gone, the pale lady remarked to the ward in general that it was such a shame that such a young girl should have to be such a long time in hospital, and what a blessing she had such a nice young man to visit her every evening.

'That's love,' she said, and Jane listened, fascinated.

Not long after that a nurse with a shiny black face came to get Jane ready for her operation, and she awoke to a terrible thirst, and a craving for the cool trickle of water down her hot, burning throat.

Afterwards, she didn't know how long afterwards, she heard footsteps echoing down the long ward, and the rasp of chairs being dragged along the wooden floor.

She opened her eyes and saw a large young man sitting by the bed on her right. His cheeks were red-veined, and his hair was cut so short that it stood up from his scalp like the bristles on a tooth-brush.

He got up to hand the nurse a bunch of flowers, and almost fell over his feet. Jane decided they were the biggest feet she had ever seen.

He was holding the freckled girl's hand as if he would never let it go, and staring into her face with an expression of such tenderness and love that Jane felt her breath catch in her sore throat.

She lay on her side, watching them, and even trying to listen to their conversation. In her dream-like state they seemed misty and unreal. The girl was smiling, and the boy was tracing the outline of her mouth with his finger.

'You're so beautiful,' Jane heard him say, and she sighed and closed her eyes, and remembered a passage she had been set to learn at school the week before . . .

They were reading *The Merchant of Venice*, and someone – she couldn't remember who – had said: 'But love is blind, and lovers cannot see . . .'

She couldn't remember any more, but she understood. Perfectly.

For the freckled girl wasn't beautiful at all. Her teeth stuck out, her hair was thin and mousey, her freckles were so big. It was because he loved her that he thought that she was so beautiful.

Jane opened her eyes and saw the girl smile a smile of pure happiness, showing all her large cream teeth. Gently, she leaned forward and tenderly stroked the young man's red-veined cheeks.

Underneath the tightly tucked-in bedclothes, Jane wriggled her toes with satisfaction.

So now she knew what love was all about! You didn't even have to be beautiful to be loved. You could be short-sighted and have fat legs, and yet some day there could be someone, somewhere, who would love you for ever and ever, amen.

There was nothing the girls at school could tell her about love. She had caught her first glimpse of it and she understood its true worth.

Now she was prepared to wait, for a year or even more . . .

To Remember for Always

It was all over so quickly. Delia couldn't believe that in such a short time anyone could *feel* as if they'd just been married.

There were no wedding bells, no bridesmaids in blue, just a handful of friends and relatives. Louise, her beautiful daughter, was dressed in what her father called her gypsy outfit, with Jonathan by her side, resplendent in peach flared trousers, with lace ruffles on his shirt.

Delia didn't exactly feel *ashamed*, more diminished. Yes, that was the word. But she hadn't interfered, she had more common sense than that. At least, as she'd said to her husband, Tom, at least they were marrying, and that was something these days.

The registrar looked as if he had a pain somewhere but was bravely putting up with it, and Peter, Jonathan's friend, who should have been a witness, hadn't got there in time, so that Tom had to step forward at the last minute, and officiate. She'd felt conspicuous in her spring suit and fluffy hat, feeling that her camel hair coat she wore for shopping would have been far more suitable.

'With a head scarf,' she'd told Tom bitterly, coming into the bedroom after seeing Louise greet Jonathan down in the hall with hilarious shrieks before taking him through into the kitchen.

'How would it look in the local paper?' she'd said, turning round from the mirror, one eye outlined in turquoise: 'The bride wore a black maxi-skirt, with a flowered blouse under a Fair Isle sleeveless tank-top, and her long hair bunched up into a hat knitted from two ounces of string-coloured rug wool.'

And Tom, wearing the dark grey suit he wore on management conference days at the office, had laughed out loud.

'At least they have their feet on the ground. Not like us, having a posh affair just to please our parents, and coming back from our honeymoon with just eighteen pounds between us in the bank.'

Delia had given him a look. 'I'm not going to say a *word*,' she'd said, and didn't.

Sitting beside Cousin Ena from Manchester in the register office, they waited their turn to go in, as two more couples, one dressed like a pantomime robber and the other in flowing robes and Indian head-bands, went in. She had maintained a dignified silence, pretending not to see Ena's face: a study of shock, intermingled with disbelief.

'Doesn't Tom mind them not being married in church, him being a sidesman, and everything?' Ena whispered, and loyal to the last ditch, Delia had stretched her mouth into what she hoped was a tolerant smile.

'They're non-believers,' she said, trying not to sound as if she cared, and Ena sniffed.

'Louise would have made a beautiful bride. Every girl should have this day, this one day, to remember for always.'

Her face crumpled, and Delia prayed she wouldn't cry. Ena had worn white, with a train seven yards long, escorted by the entire choir, with white flowers flanking the altar, and a retinue of bridesmaids in petunia pink.

That her husband had left her just two short years afterwards, didn't seem to be relevant at all. At least she'd had her day, and to prove it there was a white leather-bound album of wedding photographs, showing her throwing back her veil and laughing up at her bridegroom, their hands clasped over the handle of a knife as they cut the three-tiered cake.

Louise hadn't wanted a wedding cake.

'Just a quick cup of tea, and we'll be off,' she said. 'Once we've been done.'

No romance, no nothing. Just a few cold words mouthed by the registrar, a signing of names, a quick hand-shake, then out of the building into the rain-swept high street, with late Saturday-afternoon shoppers giving them no more than a cursory glance.

It seemed symbolic, somehow, that the house, when they returned, should feel cold and damp. Tom, with his usual streak of thriftiness, had turned the central heating down before they went out.

There wasn't going to be a honeymoon.

'Silly in February,' Louise had said. 'We'll go straight back to Jonathan's flat and get ready for the party. At the last count thirty-four were coming. We'll just have to open the windows and let them dangle their legs outside, that's all.'

Delia guessed that the majority of their friends thought it unnecessary for them to have got married at all. Apparently for Louise to have merely moved in with Jonathan, would have been more in keeping with their code of ethics.

And yet in spite of it all, she liked Jonathan. Loved him, to be honest. He had a kind and gentle face, what could be seen of it behind all that hair, and a kind and gentle manner. She knew that he loved Louise, and it was certain that Louise loved him. Surely that was what mattered?

Alone in the bedroom, leaving Tom downstairs dispensing sherry to a tearful Ena, and their tolerant friends the Evisons from across the road, Delia took off the feathered hat and sat down on the bed, fluffing her hair up again and staring at the mirror.

109

Ivory satin her gown had been, inset with long panels of lace, fastened all the way down the back with tiny covered buttons. And her veil had been lace-edged, hanging from a sparkling tiara, and framing her shoulder-length, curly hair. It had taken a whole year's clothing coupons, that and her going-away coat; a padded-shoulders, blanket-like garment. The brides-maids had worn pale blue taffeta, with white lint from the chemist sewn into their hems to make them stand out better.

Three days of a honeymoon were spent at Southport in a much blacked-out hotel, with Spam, fried for breakfast, with salad for lunch, and unbelievably turn-ing up again for dinner, flanked by powdered eggs and processed peas. They had three days of walking along a deserted promenade, holding hands, visiting the cinema twice to see *Bitter Sweet*, hearing a becurled and shiny-lipped Jeanette MacDonald sing 'I'll see you again,' to a besotted Nelson Eddy.

Not much of a honeymoon, as honeymoons go, but *romantic*. Something to remember. For always, as Ena had said.

Louise, her long hair still bundled up into the hat that would have sold as a tea-cosy on the handicrafts stall of the church bazaar, came into the room, announcing that they were off, followed by her husband, his massive moustache drooping with happiness.

Her left hand with its cheap ring – because after all, what does it *signify*? – gently touched her cheek.

'Thanks for a super wedding, Mummy. Peter's just rung up. He went to the wrong place. Finished up at the museum or something. Can't you just imagine that happening to him!'

'Just like old Pete,' said Jonathan, and surprisingly came and laid his whiskered face against hers for a moment.

Then they were gone and, standing by the window, Delia saw eight young people climb into Jonathan's four-seater beat-up car.

When Tom came in and laid a hand on her shoulder, she felt to her dismay, the prick of tears behind her eyelids.

'All went off very nicely, didn't it? Now then, there's no call for tears.'

His arms came round her, and she felt the security of his love, the warmth of his steady affection for her, and closed her eyes.

'Do you remember *our* wedding day?' she whispered. 'I mean, really remember? What I was wearing, and how the organ played, and the little talk the vicar gave us afterwards? You're glad we had that kind of day; you're glad we were *properly* married, aren't you?'

'Very glad,' said Tom.

Delia held her breath for a moment. 'What *was* I wearing?' she asked softly.

And held like that, close up against him, she couldn't see the expression on his face, couldn't see the way his eyes went blank the way they always did when she wanted him to remember something she thought was important.

'What was I wearing, Tom?'

'A long white dress,' came the prompt reply, his deep voice gaining confidence as he went on to elaborate. 'Long sleeves, with a tight waist, and pieces of lace straight down the skirt. Oh, yes, and a veil on your head with a sort of crown . . . and you carried a wreath of roses, with a horseshoe hanging from a ribbon. How's that for a good memory?'

Delia, her smile radiant, drew back from him. 'And you're glad we married in church and everything?'

'And everything,' he said, and gently pulled her to her feet, steering her firmly towards the door, and downstairs to where cousin Ena was drinking a cup of tea in a refined sort of way.

And as the two women went into a long discourse on the way things have changed, and what a lot the young people are missing. Tom sat quietly in his chair, his pipe going nicely, reminding himself to have a few quiet words with his daughter's husband.

He would tell him that in twenty-nine years from now, he would be expected to remember every detail of his wife's wedding outfit and *without* a framed photograph on her dressing-table to prompt him, things might prove just a bit difficult.

Then, remembering what Louise had been wearing that day, he laughed out loud, causing Ena to remark that she was glad someone was amused.

Dominic

Rose had been married for five years, and had loved her husband Ben for slightly longer, but the shameful thing was that never, even for a moment, had she felt about him the way she had felt about the other one.

When she looked back it was with complete and utter amazement that the rational, well-adjusted woman she considered herself to be had behaved with an abandonment that in retrospect bordered on the wild.

It wasn't that Rose had suddenly seen Dominic, the other one, across a crowded room – or on the other side of a crowded street – and wondered how she could possibly have seen anything in him; nothing like that. She had never seen him again from the time they parted.

The disillusionment went far deeper than that . . .

They had met for the first time at the office Christmas dinner dance.

'You're the Old Man's secretary?' he'd asked, bringing a drink over to her. 'I believe we are sitting together at dinner.'

Then he introduced himself and said he was no longer London based, but down from their Scottish branch on a temporary basis.

And it happened – just like that, with pealing bells and soaring violins, with the tall fair man smiling down at her as faces, voices faded away like drifting ectoplasm.

'You are very lovely,' he told Rose before the fish course was whisked away, and she almost forgot herself enough to tell him that so was he.

Everything Dominic said made her smile. She could

feel her face widen into happy creases, and little witticisms she had thought she was incapable of bubbled from her lips.

When he dropped her at the flat she shared with two girls who worked for the BBC, she got into the lift, pressed the button for the fourth floor, and closed her eyes in an ecstasy that would have been more appropriate had she been sitting on a cloud ascending into heaven.

The reflection in her dressing-table mirror startled her. Her hair was curling over her forehead in just the way she always wished it would. Her eyes sparkled, and her cheeks glowed as if they'd been painted with a blush of coral.

She, who was not remotely beautiful, was as beautiful as only a woman in love can be.

And the shameful thing – the first of the shameful things – was that, as the days went by and he did not ring, she telephoned *him*.

Her hand shook as she dialled the number; then when she was put through to his extension, her heart began to beat so loudly that she put a hand to her breast, and when she heard his voice, her own came out so soft it sounded alien to her.

'I've been so busy. I was going to give you a ring,' he said, and even if she had recognised the half-reluctance in his voice she would have ignored it.

'How *are* you?' she asked him, and it was no idle question. She literally wanted to know how he was, how he was feeling at that particular moment; even if he was not saying the things she wanted to hear, it was enough that he was there at the other end.

'Do you enjoy Alan Ayckbourn's plays? There's one on at my local little theatre. I've got two tickets for Friday. I thought maybe you are feeling lonely – I mean with not really knowing anyone down here . . .'

It was humiliating, and after she had replaced the

receiver she was actually trembling; but he had said that he would come.

And in the four days in between Rose gave her brown hair a colour rinse, washed it out again, and bought a new green woollen dress.

Then on the night, because she was twenty minutes early, she went into a rather sleazy café across the street from the small theatre and took a cup of coffee over to a table by the window. She bought a packet of cigarettes from the machine, even though she had not smoked for months, then smoked two – one after the other in jerky puffs.

She closed her eyes and prayed to God more earnestly than she had done since Confirmation, and when she opened them she saw that exactly on time, Dominic was there.

He touched her hair in the tiny foyer, and that simple gesture of affection – it had to be affection – lifted her spirit to the stars. She sat beside him on the third row from the back, and his nearness blotted out all concentration.

With aching longing she placed her hand in an inviting gesture on the arm of her chair; but he did not take it, and later he told her that he had been living with a girl called Janet for the past year, and hoped to marry her at the end of the summer.

And the girl she used to be would have been dismayed, singed with a lick of jealousy, but the girl she had become dismissed the far-away Janet as if she had never existed.

'I've never felt like this before,' she told him when they said good-night and he kissed her with more than a show of reluctance. 'I don't know you, but I think I love you. How can that be?'

'You are very lovable; and if I had met you first, if

things were different . . .' He bent his head and kissed her again with considerably more enthusiasm this time.

She was an intelligent, reasonably liberated young woman of today. She was capable of self-analysis, of seeing herself and a problem straight on. But from then on she moved through the next few months like a zombie from one infrequent meeting to the next.

She became a sucker for television advertisements for shining hair, for scents guaranteed to ensnare the man of any girl's dreams. She identified with the sickly lyrics of pop songs, and cried real tears each time he let her down.

And the way it ended was indicative of the whole wasted time of her loving. 'I have to go back to Scotland. My time down here has ended sooner than I thought,' he told her. He was speaking from his office, using what she had come to know as his telephone voice; then as she stood numbed and disbelieving, he whispered: 'I shall always keep a corner of my heart especially for you.'

He actually said that, and she hugged the trite words to her as if they were sealed in a hot-water bottle to be held warm against her in the dark days she knew would come.

And to her surprise the days of desolation did not last as long as she had been convinced they would. It was as though she woke up one day and realised that her mourning had no substance.

When she met Ben, the man she was to marry, there were no soaring violins, no pealing bells. He was merely a man she liked and respected, and when he telephoned her she spoke to him with a quiet pleasure at hearing his voice – nothing else.

Their relationship took a sweet and ordered course, and sometimes her happiness took her unawares as if

116

it had been slowly creeping up on her, unheralded and unsung.

A man without sentimentality was her Ben, a man who would never have referred to a corner of his heart, for the simple reason that he knew full well the heart was formed as a series of curves.

Practical, honest – as honest as she, and totally immune to what his Northern upbringing would have considered to be 'flarchy' talk – he nevertheless was bewildered one day when his bride-to-be said with feeling: 'Oh, dearest, I am so glad I love you without ever having been in love with you.'

'There's a difference?' asked Ben.

'There's no comparison,' Rose told him on a contented sigh . . .

Visiting Time

It is now almost seven o'clock – visiting time, and all the mothers in the ward are sitting up straight in bed, waiting for the moment when their husbands come in. Husbands carrying flowers and grapes, and clean nighties in paper bags. They'll kiss their wives, and lean over the glass-sided cots, making fatherly noises at their babies, and they'll swear that they're managing on their own just fine.

That's how it always is at seven o'clock visiting time, and last night I cried behind the magazine I was holding up in front of my face.

Tonight you're coming to see me, Mum and Dad, and I know how thrilled you are with your first grandchild.

I've seen the way you look at her, and adore her, lying there, rounded and perfect, wrapped up like a cocoon in her swaddling blanket, her long dark eyelashes lying sweetly on her soft, pale cheeks.

You've been marvellous to me, both of you. I'll never be able to thank you enough for the way you've been.

I didn't have to tell you, Mum, that something was worrying me sick during those first awful weeks. You *knew*. And when I told you that there was no question of me getting married; that he was already married; that I wasn't even going to tell him I was going to have a baby, you cried as if your heart would break.

And watching you, I think mine broke a little too.

So many times I've wanted to tell you just the way it was, but as close as we are, I've never been able to talk to you about things *like that*. See, I can't even say the word 'sex' to you in my thoughts . . . But in those early days, I saw you watching me, I knew you were wondering just how your well brought-up daughter could possibly have done a thing like that.

Oh, Mum, it was all too easy. Too many drinks at a party, the intimacy of a parked car in a dark lane; arms holding me close, the feeling of power when a man, especially an older man, murmured words of longing, pleading with me. And the tenderness flooding me with an emotion I'd never experienced before, an emotion I'll never understand, not if I live to be a hundred.

When you saw that I was determined to stand on my own two feet, you were marvellous, not caring what the neighbours thought, or at least, not letting me see that you cared.

'I'll go on working for as long as I can, then when the baby comes, I'll put it in a nursery and go back to the office,' I said.

'You'll do no such thing! What are grannies for?' you said then, and I knew just how wonderful you were . . .

The first proud father is coming through the door, walking down the ward, carrying a brown paper parcel, a bunch of exhausted anemones, and a glossy magazine. His wife lifts her face for his kiss, and although I can't hear her, I know she's telling him about her baby being sick this morning. He touches her cheek with his finger, and I know he's telling her not to worry. She smiles, and together they lean over the cot by the side of her bed, adoring their baby.

And I realise that if I panic, and I know I *will* panic – she's so little and helpless – there'll be no husband to trail his finger down my cheek, soothing me with words of love.

The husband of the girl in the bed next to mine comes in now, with black splashes of rain on his leather jacket.

'It's just started to pour,' he tells her, and before she can stop him, he goes to the cot and picks up his little son.

His wife is horrified. 'You'll wet him,' she scolds, 'and if Sister catches you, there'll be trouble!'

Her husband winks at me. 'We're not frightened of any old Sister, are we, old son?' he whispers before tucking the baby back into his cot with surprising tenderness.

I look away, my throat tightening with the tears I mustn't shed.

Not in front of Mum and Dad. Not after the way they've been.

I can see them now, coming down the long corridor. I can see them through the glass door, Mum walking a little ahead of Dad. She's turning to ask him something, and he nods and points to a paper bag, and I know they've remembered to bring me a cardigan because I told them I was cold in the mornings.

They are kind, and sweet, and loving, and I smile at them, and they lean over the baby, and Mum says again that she looks exactly like I did when I was a baby.

I *know* just how lucky I am, but I wonder if they realise what it's going to be like with a new baby in their neat and well-ordered house? A baby who screams in the night, and grows into a toddler, leaving sticky finger marks on the doors and new chintz covers they're so proud of.

My mum was thirty-five when I was born, and I don't need telling that they are too old to start again.

My baby starts to cry, and Mum lifts her and gives her to me, and I hold her in my arms, and her little mouth is sucking on nothing, and her head turns from side to side, searching for her feed.

I give her my finger to hold, and her grip is unbelievably tight for such a new baby, and her eyelids quiver, but she is going off to sleep again.

Mum is putting my cardigan away in my locker, and Dad is patting the pocket in his coat where he keeps his pipe and tobacco pouch. I know he is dying for a smoke . . .

I am not going to cry. I will myself not to cry, and I smile and talk to them, but the tears are there.

When Mum and Dad have gone I hide my face underneath the sheet, and let the tears roll down my cheeks, and I feel the salt taste of them on my lips.

I'll manage. We'll manage. I've got to get through.

But no one, not one single person, told me how lonely, how *desperately* lonely I would be . . .

Dream of Tomorrow

Her voice is kitten-soft, and a strand of her long hair, escaping from the little crocheted cap, tickles his chin as he holds her close to him.

'Close your eyes,' she orders, and because he loves her very much, he does as he is told . . . he closes his eyes.

'We are standing on the balcony of our room in an hotel – an hotel overlooking the Mediterranean. The sea is a spread of black silk, and the sky is patterned thick with twinkling stars.

'I am wearing a glamorous nightie, see-through and pale blue,' she giggles, 'and resting on a ledge in front of us are two glasses of champagne. We are on our honeymoon, and when you hold me tight like this, I protest a little, because we have been sunbathing all day, and my back is sore.'

A thin drift of drizzle, freezing cold drizzle, spiked with particles of snow, blows round them in the doorway where they shelter, and the tyres of a passing car make a soft, sad, swishing sound.

But she is quite oblivious to everything but her dream.

'We could go back to your house, but your father doesn't like me,' he says. 'He thinks you are too young to have a boyfriend, and your mother thinks because my hair is long I must have rape in mind.'

'We have been dancing,' she whispers, 'outside on the terrace, and a gorgeous Italian boy with a guitar and a sob in his throat has sung to us as we danced, and we've drunk a whole bottle of wine – between us, of course.'

He kisses her gently.

'Gosh, your little nose is as cold as ice,' he grumbles.

'It is two o'clock in the morning, but the air is as warm as on a lovely English summer's day. We are going to sleep on top of the bedclothes, with not even a sheet to cover us,' she tells him, and he sighs.

'We could go back to our house, but they will be watching television, and we will have to sit there with them, and my father will make his awful jokes, and my mother will tell you, nicely of course, that I ought to be studying, that it's no wonder I failed my last exam, and you'll know she's blaming you, and you'll go all shy and not say a word. My mother thinks you have no personality at all,' he adds, cruelly.

'We were married yesterday morning,' she goes on, 'in the church I was christened in, and after the reception we caught a plane, and we flew so high the sky was the blue of heaven, and beneath us the clouds were like a drifting sea of cotton wool.'

'If we'd had another coffee, we could have stayed in the café in the warm. I bet there are no two people on earth who can make a cup of coffee last as long as we can,' he says, now facing reality.

'We stand there, sipping champagne, and you say it's time we went to bed, and I think how great you look in your smart shortie pyjamas.'

She thinks for a moment. 'Dark green, piped with brown.'

He stamps his feet. 'My blinkin' feet have gone dead. It's all right for you in those high boots and that long, maxi thing. Lend me a bit of your scarf, it's long enough for both of us.'

Gently, and with infinite tenderness, she takes a length of the purple crocheted scarf, and wraps it round his throat with a motherly gesture, and they stand

124

entwined, staring lovingly into each other's faces and studying every feature.

He thinks she must be the most beautiful girl in the world, and he tells her so.

She has taken off one glove, and with fingers stiff with cold, she gently traces the outline of his mouth.

'It is *so* hot,' she tells him, 'but not sweaty hot, and all along the sea-front there are coloured lights, twinkling and swaying in the soft breeze, and tomorrow we are going to swim in the sea, and lie on towels on the rocks, and I am going to make a little paper cone for your nose, because already it is turning red, and somehow I don't think I will be able to love you quite so much with the skin peeling from it, and dangling down in masses of little shreds.'

He holds her away from him, as far as the woollen scarf will allow.

'Do you have any idea of how long it will be before I have passed my engineering examinations? Do you realise how many years we have before us of standing in windy doorways like this, freezing to death because we have nowhere in the world where we can be alone?

'You'll meet someone else. When you leave school and go to a training college in September, you'll meet someone else – perhaps a bloke with a car, and he'll have money to take you out for meals in smart restaurants, real nosh-ups, starting with prawn cocktails, and you'll forget about me.'

'I don't like prawn cocktail,' she tells him gravely.

A policeman walks past, shining his torch briefly on them for a moment, and then he passes on.

The winter wind, blowing straight from the plains of Siberia he could swear, lifts a bedraggled sheet of news-paper, and it twines itself round his legs.

Her eyes, carefully drawn in with black eyeliner, and

ringed with startling white eye-shadow, look enormous in the darkness, and with a smothered groan he pulls her close to him so that their bodies fuse, and through his duffle coat and thick-knit sweater, his heart beats so loudly he is sure that she can hear it.

And then he does close his eyes, and his voice, when he begins to speak, is muffled with dreams.

'I think we'll go into our room now,' he whispers, 'but we'll leave the balcony window open, and we'll sit up in bed, and drink the rest of the champagne, and the moon will shine in. You forgot the moon.'

She is happy now. He can tell by the sound of her young voice that she is happy.

'My apologies to the moon,' she says, laughing happily.

And their kiss is all that a kiss should be, promising everything, guaranteeing nothing, and as a nearby cinema disgorges its audience on to the slippery pavement, stupefied with its weekly ration of sex, violence, and full frontal nudity, they huddle closer together, oblivious to it all, a little tiddly from the sparkling champagne they've drunk, their bodies tingling with sunburn, beneath the wonderful, soft and velvety warmth of a Mediterranean sky.

Unknown Admirer

After they said goodbye – goodbye for ever – she gave herself until Christmas to forget him, then extended it by a month. And by the time February came in, she had at last accepted the fact that Andrew no longer loved her.

Then, on Saturday the twelfth – arriving two days early – she received a Valentine card. Unsigned, of course, but when she read the verse, she knew immediately that Andrew had sent it.

It wasn't one of the modern, off-beat, sick verse kinds of Valentine, but the real old Victorian type, in the form of a lace-trimmed heart, with a glory of wild summer flowers blooming round its rim.

'Here's flowers for you,' the verse on the inside began, and immediately Carole remembered.

A warm summer day, a country lane, dust seeping through the narrow straps of her sandals; the sun was warm as a blessing, on the wild flowers of the hedgerows.

Andrew had picked a small nosegay, tiny blue bells, star-like pink miniature daisies, and feathery 'bread and cheese'.

'Here's flowers for you,' he'd said and as she held out her hands for them, he'd pulled her to him and kissed her with slow, sweet deliberation.

'I love you,' he said. 'For ever,' he'd said. And she believed him.

Then what had happened to their love?

He had remembered, or at least when he had seen the card, the words on it had reminded him, and his remembering could mean only one thing . . .

And yet, as she dialled his number, she was filled with sudden apprehension. For whatever was she going to say to him?

Her job as receptionist in a Park Lane hotel had given her poise and confidence, but the sound of his voice could turn her into a gabbling idiot.

The ringing tone stopped and she spoke quickly, before her courage failed her: 'Andrew. Carole here,' she said. There was a small hesitation, then incredulous surprise in his voice.

'Carole! How nice to hear from you. How *are* you?'

At the remembered, well-loved sound of his voice, she closed her eyes, actually swaying a little, but she willed her voice to remain steady.

'I'm fine. How are you?'

'Fine. Where are you ringing from? The hotel?'

'No. It's my Saturday off. I'm ringing from the flat, from home.'

She felt him smile.

'Sitting on the floor, with the red telephone beside you on the rug?'

She felt an upsurge of delight. He hadn't forgotten that either. She glanced at the Valentine card on the table beside her and loved him for remembering.

He had remembered something else too. 'How's Ross?' he said.

She wouldn't get angry. She had told him and told him that Ross was just a lonely American on a six-month business trip, and staying at the hotel. It was her job to befriend him, she'd said.

'If there's one thing I can't stand it's possessiveness,' she'd told him during that last quarrel.

'And if there's one thing I just can't stand, it's flighty women,' he had said.

'Ross went back to the States six weeks ago,' she said quietly.

'And now you're missing him,' Andrew said, and it

wasn't a question, more a statement of fact. 'Now you're lonely. Is that why you telephoned me?'

She *wouldn't* get angry. He had made the first move, hadn't he? She couldn't bear it if they quarrelled again, and the card with its unspoken message made her pride a foolish thing.

'I love *you*,' she said. 'You, only you. You must have known.'

He didn't speak and the silence went on until, her heart pounding, she replaced the receiver and picked up the card, tears welling up and running down her cheeks . . .

When Andrew came, she was lying on her bed, drained, empty and sad after her paroxysm of weeping. Not caring how she looked, she opened the door. He stood there, dark and serious, not saying a word, just staring at her.

Then she was in his arms and he was kissing her, wildly and passionately, and she was thanking him for the card, saying how wonderful it was that he had found it, with the message that told her all she had longed to know.

And held close to him, she was unable to see the bewilderment in his eyes.

Never in his life had he sent a Valentine card, nor was he ever likely to, but with all his being, with every fibre of his soul, he thanked the unknown sender, knowing that he would be grateful to him for the rest of his life . . .

The Comforters

She was a perfect stranger, and yet in ten minutes flat, over the sipping of our respective coffees in the Copper Kettle, she had told me what was virtually the story of her life.

At least the story of her life from the moment when her daughter, almost overnight if she was to be believed, had turned from a sweet, cooperative little girl into a belligerent, uncooperative teenager.

'It's the boys she goes around with,' she said. 'Long hair, scruffy jeans, no ambition . . . and the one she's friendly with at the moment . . .' Her eyes glistened with what were surely tears of frustration. 'And after all the advantages we've given her – a good education, a nice home. It hurts me, actually hurts.'

She sighed deeply.

'It's a phase,' I soothed. 'They all go through it. Take my son, now.' At the very thought of him I found myself plunging into a kind of mild maniacal depression, but loyalty made me smile bravely. 'He's just started his apprenticeship with a marvellous firm, and has every opportunity to do well, and last week he brought a girl home . . .'

I shuddered, and suggested that we had another coffee.

'The girl he's friendly with at the moment,' I confided, 'smokes, and doesn't seem to have a thought in her empty little mind beyond how fast she can spend my son's money.'

I waited until the waiter had placed our second cups in front of us, and retreated out of earshot. 'And the books he reads . . .'

My friend across the table dropped a spoonful of brown sugar into her coffee, and sadly stirred it round and round. 'I know,' she said. 'The other day when I was making my daughter's bed I found a book beneath her pillow, and I sat down and read a page or two.'

She actually blushed. 'Whoever wrote that book had but one thought in his mind. And I wouldn't be at all surprised if that boy hadn't lent it to her. My husband says I ought to forbid him the house, but I can't agree.'

'You can't do that. Forbid isn't a word they accept these days.'

'You let them bring their friends home, and hope that when they see them against their own backgrounds they will see for themselves how unsuitable they are.'

'Do you think it ever works?'

She sighed again, and glared so fiercely at a camel-coated shopper intent on joining us at our table that she moved hastily away to a table in the dark by the cash register.

'Nothing works. You can only hope that the way you've brought them up will have had some effect in the long run.'

She twisted her gloves into a string. 'I can't get through to my daughter at all since she started going around with this boy. We used to have little chats, you know, woman to woman, but not now.'

'I know,' I said. 'And when this girl sits on the settee you can see half-way to her navel.'

'His hair touches his collar,' she said, passing me a cigarette, which I accepted, feeling I needed it, although I'd stopped smoking for my New Year resolution.

She took a long and nervous drag. 'We had friends in the other evening, and she brought him in – they'd been to the pictures, and I felt so sorry for my husband. These friends, they were business colleagues, you know?'

I said that I knew.

'*Their* daughter's at a teachers' training college,' she went on, 'and engaged to a nice young man going in for the ministry. Lovely boy, lovely hair.'

'Short back and sides?' I suggested, but she smiled tolerantly. 'Not quite, but nothing like this boy my daughter brought home. If she has no respect for herself, at least she ought to have some for us.'

'But they haven't,' I said, and sadly she agreed.

'It's comforting to know that someone else is going through the same thing,' she said as we argued mildly about paying the bill and leaving a tip. 'It has been nice to talk about it to someone totally unconnected, if you know what I mean.'

'Even if it hasn't done any good,' I smiled.

We gathered our gloves and shopping bags together.

'When I look at her, so sweet and lovely, walking out with this boy, I feel we've failed somehow,' she said, reluctant to go.

'When I see my son with this girl I feel actually sick,' I said, exaggerating only a little.

Together we walked to the cash desk, still arguing about the bill, and outside, as traffic streamed towards the Town Hall, we exchanged coins, even splitting the tip fifty-fifty, as strangers will.

She consulted her watch. 'I'm meeting my daughter just across the road. She comes out of work around this time, and we can travel home together.'

'That's nice,' I said, and mesmerised by her friendliness, and at a lull in the traffic, crossed the road with her, and stood for a moment admiring a window decked out in singing colours of spring yellows and greens.

I held out my hand. 'It has been nice meeting you,' I said again, but she ignored my outstretched hand and froze as she stared past me over my shoulder.

'She's here,' she said, 'and guess who's with her?'

133

Her mouth tightened into a grim line, and her eyes behind her upswept spectacles flashed fire.

'That boy?' I hissed, with her every inch of the way, and quite reluctant to go until my curiosity had been satisfied.

'They're crossing the road now, with their arms round each other,' she whispered dramatically.

'I'll leave you to it then,' I said, and started to walk away; but after all she'd said I just had to turn round and see for myself.

I saw them straight away. They were coming straight towards us, now holding hands, a tall, dark boy, and a pint-sized girl with long fair hair, and a barely thigh-length white skirt.

'I swear his hair's grown a couple of inches since last week,' my friend said, 'and surely he hasn't been to work in jeans?'

They stopped in front of us, the tall dark boy, and the little fair-haired girl, still swinging hands, then they turned to each other and laughed out loud.

'Well, fancy you two knowing each other,' the girl said, from underneath her hair. 'Sorry if I've kept you waiting, Mummy.'

'Well, hallo, Mum,' said my son, smiling.

Fancy Seeing You Here

She saw him again, as she had dreamed she would do one day. Suddenly, unexpectedly, walking towards her, his face still tanned from the summer's sun, his hair just a shade too long, ragged round his ears, thick and black, badly in need of a trim.

'Hello, you!' he said, grinning down at her in the remembered teasing way. 'I can't believe it! What are you doing out this way?'

And she told him breathlessly that her boss had asked her to deliver a manuscript personally to his publisher because he'd missed a deadline. 'And you,' she said. 'What are you doing round here?'

'My car broke down and it will be an hour before it's ready,' he told her. As he took her arm she blushed and remarked once more on the amazing coincidence; and remembering what a romantic she was, he said it was fate.

'Meant to be,' he said, and they stopped and stared at each other in delight as if a miracle had enfolded there in the Edgware Road.

And suddenly she was happy again and not the disillusioned girl she had become. Two whole years younger; twenty and not twenty-two, walking along by his side, oblivious to the passing crowds, hearing his voice, watching the way he smiled, their steps matching, their thoughts as one. The way it used to be.

'You are like my other half,' he had said in the days of their loving.

And she had replied in all seriousness, 'I *am* your other half.'

135

He was leading her now into a Chinese restaurant across the road, taking it for granted that she would lunch with him, and she felt tender towards him because he had remembered her fondness for Chinese food.

And it was all so quick, so wonderful, so simply meant to be, that she had scarcely caught her breath before the almond-eyed waiter had whisked the huge red-backed menus away and brought their drinks. A beer for him and the driest of sherries for her. He'd remembered that too.

She stared at him; she could not take her eyes away from his face, from the long sensitive curve of his mouth and the suspicion of a cleft in his chin. No, she wasn't married, she told him, and when he said that he wasn't either, she had to close her eyes for a moment in an overwhelming relief.

She wouldn't ask him why he hadn't married her, the other one, the girl he'd met at a party and left her for. The tall long-legged girl with the Purdie hair-do and the pale blue dress falling in handkerchief points just the right fashionable length from the floor. It was enough that they had found each other again in such an unbelievable way.

She marvelled at the miracle as the little steaming dishes were set before them, succulent chicken and prawns, mushrooms and slivers of beef, and they pushed their spoons away as he beckoned the waiter over and requested chop-sticks, the way they had always done before.

'Are you still working for the same firm?' she asked him, and he told her that he was, but that now he was one step higher and had acquired a secretary called Mabel.

'With tight, grey curls and trouble with her feet,' he said, and she couldn't believe it.

'A secretary of your own?' Her brown eyes were

round, and he spoilt it just a little by admitting that Mabel was shared by three other reps.

'So I own only one quarter of Mabel,' he said sadly and, sighing deeply, helped her to more rice.

'Two years,' he said. 'Tell me what you've been doing for two whole years.'

Nonchalantly, she replied: 'Oh, this and that.' Pride prevented her from saying that since he left her it had seemed as if time stood still. Not still with the magic of something happening all the time. Oh, not that. Still with the heaviness of heartache, the growing knowledge that no-one could ever hope to measure up to him.

'He has ruined you for everyone else,' her mother had said dramatically, but she had been right. For she would sit across the table from someone else, and dance with someone else, and unkindly substitute him for them so that they realised she had gone far away from them.

Once, about a year ago, she had suddenly stopped typing and, reaching for the telephone, had dialled his number, her fingers moving of their own volition. Then, when he'd answered and she'd heard his voice, she had replaced the receiver and buried her face in her hands.

'I am behaving like a girl of fourteen, not a woman of twenty-one,' she had scolded herself. And she had never done it again . . .

'Did you have a party when you were twenty-one?' he asked her then, and she stared at him, not really surprised, because he had always been able to read her thoughts.

'Yes,' she told him quietly. 'I had a party. My mother can't resist a party, and there were aunties and uncles and cousins at one end of the room, and me and my friends at the other.' She smiled so that a dimple came and went at the side of her mouth, and he watched her, enchanted.

137

'And never the twain met, all the evening,' she said and, because she was so happy at finding him again, she leaned against him for a moment, smiling into his shoulder.

This girl, he thought, a lump coming into his throat and almost choking him so that it was difficult to swallow the food, this lovely girl I hurt so much, telling her abruptly as we walked down a crowded Saturday evening street together that I wouldn't be seeing her again. Exchanging her adoration for the shallow physical love of a girl who wasn't fit to hold a candle to her.

He bit his lip as he remembered the way she had walked into a hedge, the privet hedge of someone's house, because of the tears that were blinding her.

'It's quite all right,' she had whispered. 'I understand.'

And then she had told him that she would rather walk the rest of the way home herself, if he didn't mind. And he'd watched her go, her head down, walking unsteadily as if she were drunk, and he'd hated her for making him feel like an unfeeling rotter.

'This time I'm never going to let you go,' he said, taking the chop-sticks from her so that he could hold both her hands in his own. 'How long does it take to make all the arrangements for a wedding?'

No, there was nothing whatsoever wrong with the food, they told the waiter with the almond eyes. It was delicious, simply delicious, but they . . . it was just that they . . .

And by the way he smiled on them, bowing them out of the restaurant, accepting the quite outrageous tip, it was obvious that he understood.

They parted at the entrance to the tube station. But only for a few hours, he promised. He would come round and see her that very evening. There was so much to say, a whole two years of wasted life to make

138

up for, and he kissed her a temporary goodbye by the newspaper stand.

'Now you'll have to believe in miracles,' she said before she ran lightly down the steps. 'Because how could it be other than a miracle the way we've met today? I've never been in this particular district before in the whole of my life.'

His own voice was full of wonder. 'And for me to choose this bit of Edgware Road to walk down, just killing time . . .'

They shook their heads then kissed again before saying a tender goodbye.

And as he turned and walked quickly to the bus-stop to stand in line, he sent up a prayer of forgiveness for what was surely only the whitest of white lies?

For how could he tell her that, missing her like hell, he had used up three days of his leave trying to bump into her 'accidentally'?

How could he tell her that he had waited outside her boss's house, lurking behind a tree, had followed her to the tube station, stalking her like a television private eye?

She wanted to believe in miracles. Okay then, she could have her miracle. And for the rest of her life he would let her believe that the fate she set such store by had stepped right in and caused them to meet in the busy Edgware Road.

'Out of all the hundreds and thousands of people in London,' she would tell her children, 'out of all the hundreds and thousands of streets in the world, there he was, your father, walking towards me, just as I had dreamed he would one day.'

The red bus trundled to a stop and he swung himself aboard.

Sometimes even the most shining of miracles needed a little help. Well, didn't they?

139

What Kind of Girl Am I?

When you're twenty-five, and you've been in love four times, and each time it's come to nothing, and you live all alone and are considering acquiring a cat, buying little parcels of fish for it on your way home from the office – well it's time you admitted that you could have a problem.

A psychiatrist would label me as suffering from a common quirk of mentality. 'Lack of identity' it's called in the trade . . .

I am the first to admit that I've never 'found myself', and the reason is simple. I haven't known where to look!

But Mark, my latest boyfriend, had begun to stare at me with a questioning expression in his blue eyes – a look I knew only too well – and I was just waiting for him to tell me that he thought we were getting too serious about each other, or that with the world the way it was, there wasn't room for intense relationships.

It frightened me, because I knew that if he left me, I would be so devastated, I'd be in danger of kicking the cat I'd thought to replace him with. The whole thing came to a head during my lunch-hour, when I was rushing frantically round the shops, trying to buy a dress to wear that same evening, when he was taking me out to dinner.

'There are things we must talk about, Sylvia,' he'd said on the telephone. And I knew it was the beginning of the end.

So there I was, in a little under-heated cubicle in a Regent Street store, all zipped up into what the assistant called an after-six cocktail dress, studying myself in the full-length mirror.

My hair is pale, my eyes light brown, my skin pallid, and the dress was beige. But when I told the assistant I looked anonymous, she patted her silver-grey hair, and sighed at me.

'That dress is *just you*, madam.'

'You're right,' I said, but I didn't mean what she meant. And sure of a sale, she went off happily, giving me, she said, a few minutes to think it over.

Usually, when I'm told a dress is 'just me', I'm thrown into a panic, because I haven't the slightest idea what 'me' is!

Take my name. Sylvia.

I was left at one week old, neatly wrapped in a white shawl, on the doorstep of a children's home, with a desperate little note pinned to my nightie, imploring the finders to take good care of me. And because Matron's name happened to be Sylvia, that was what I was landed with. From then on I lived with a series of foster parents, and although all efforts had been made to find my mother, no-one had claimed me. So at the age of eighteen, I found myself a job, and a bed-sitter in London.

It's a well-known fact that some people wake up in the mornings and ask themselves seriously: 'Why am I here?' or 'What is it all about?' But I never did that.

I would wake in the mornings asking myself just one question: '*Who* am I?'

And because there was no-one who could tell me, and to compensate, I suppose, I started to take on, chameleon-like, the colour and personality of the person I happened to be with.

When I was nineteen, there was Roger, and Roger was a car fanatic. So I had gone around with him, pretending to be fascinated with oil leaks and mythical

142

knocks in engines. It was for him that I'd bought my shaggy coat – the trendiest thing in my wardrobe – so I'd be warm during all-night rallies. Then one day Roger realised that the colour of the car seats was the only thing that interested me.

Adrian had been a health food fanatic, and I'd forced myself to eat repulsively nutty roasts, and learned how to cut up radishes so that they resembled roses in full bloom.

Then one day he'd called round unexpectedly, and caught me tucking into a pork chop, flanked by chips cooked in lard. We had a row, and he called me a 'sham'.

Conrad played rugger, and said things like: 'Cricket is not so much a game as a way of life', so I'd spent one entire summer sitting outside various pavilions on deckchairs, knitting him white sweaters that came down to his knees. Then a whole winter was spent jogging on the spot in muddy fields, trying to keep warm.

But I gave myself away one day, when, as we discussed the Twickenham International, I inadvertently called a 'scrum' an 'over'. And that was that.

Which brings me to Mark.

Mark has quite a mundane job in one of the Ministries, signing forms in triplicate all day, but, perhaps to make up for this, he has an avid interest in what is called the Arts.

The first time I met him was at a cocktail party, given by a girl in the flat across from the one I'd progressed to as my meagre salary increased.

That evening I'd worn a long dress in black, with a high, throat-hugging collar, and while I was delicately nibbling a little triangular-shaped biscuit, topped with

143

a slice of hard-boiled egg and the tail end of an anchovy, he had told me I reminded him of Jane Eyre.

'I think every page of the Brontës' books are quotable, don't you?' he'd said.

Mesmerised by the brilliant blue of his eyes, and wanting to please him, I'd said: 'Oh, yes,' then prayed he wouldn't ask me to recite a page there and then.

I'm not ignorant. Not by any means. As recently as four years ago, I'd started to read the first volume of the *Brothers Karamazov*, and even got as far as page one hundred and twenty-seven before leaving off.

But of course, being the way I am, because I'd fallen in love with him on the spot, I'd been Jane Eyre ever since.

I found myself staring critically at the beige dress, trying to visualise her, Jane, in it. It was certainly demure enough, and with my cameo brooch, a recent birthday present from Mark, and my blonde hair parted in the middle, and combed back smoothly on each side . . .

'Yes, I'll take it,' I said and, as it was being wrapped up, I wandered round the store and saw a row of glittering waistcoats, designed to be worn over flecked tweed plus-fours. I thought they were fabulous, and hesitated, actually fingering one in my size, but then I turned away.

No. Who in their wildest imagination could see Jane Eyre wearing gear like that? The very thought was enough to make the entire Brontë family turn over in their wind-swept graves.

Mark seemed preoccupied when he picked me up that evening, and when he saw the dress, and I told him it was new, he said: 'Very nice.'

Well, what had I expected? A satisfying wolf-whistle? I was quite sure that Jane would never have expected Mr Rochester to do anything so vulgar as to whistle.

And no-one could have compared Mark with Mr

Rochester. He's not the dark brooding type. Mark is good-natured, broad-shouldered, with a twinkle in his eye.

'I've found a new place to eat,' he said. 'The kind of place you like, Sylvia. Quiet and discreet, where I can talk to you.'

I nodded, meekly, ready to fall in with anything he suggested, but my heart did a downward flip.

We got a seat at a little table in an alcove, and he reached across and took my hand.

'Sylvia,' he began, 'I don't know how to put this . . .'

His voice was low, but each table was so cleverly segregated that he could have been making the most improper of suggestions to me, or even confessing to brutal murder, without the slightest chance of being overheard.

'Yes?' I said gently.

By now, his other hand had reduced his bread-roll to crumbs.

'As I said, I don't even know how to put this; I'm not even clear about it in my own mind. But well, I have to admit that I don't know you any better now than the night we first met.'

He arranged the mutilated bread-roll into neat little piles of crumbs. 'It's as though I'm taking out a shadow, an insubstantial nothing. If I'm happy, then you're happy. If I'm feeling low, then you even go as far as to sigh with me. Sylvia, don't you have any feelings of your own?'

He picked up the menu. 'If I said I wasn't hungry right now, that I'd decided against eating after all, then you'd get up like a lamb, and follow me out of this place, swearing you didn't want to eat either. I love you, but with love should come respect, and how can I respect a girl who tries so hard to please me?'

It was a good speech, even for a man who can quote

145

whole pages of the Bronte novels. As we sat there, staring at each other, a waiter appeared at our table, but Mark waved him away, asking him politely to come back later.

'I'm waiting for an answer, Sylvia,' he said.

I fingered the cameo brooch at my throat, wondering what Jane would have said, then suddenly I came to a decision.

'Mark,' I said, and my voice came out more loudly than I'd intended. 'Would you really like to know the kind of person I am?'

'Very much indeed,' Mark said quietly.

So then I told him about my childhood, about the way there wasn't a single person in the whole world I could call my own. How it had taken me a long time to realise I was so insecure, and I'd thought that only by trying to please everyone I met, could I expect them to like me in return.

By now Jane had disappeared back into the pages of a novel, where she belonged. Now I was being my true self and I wanted to make a clean breast of it all.

'That play we went to last week,' I went on, 'the one where the entire cast sat around on the stage, talking very distinctly to each other about life, and moaning beautifully about the fact that they couldn't identify?'

'Marvellous,' said Mark. But I shook my head.

'I was bored stiff.'

Mark's eyebrows flew to his hairline, but I hadn't finished yet.

'And do you know the kind of thing I *really* like to read?'

He shook his head.

'Well, last week I read a fascinating article telling me why Liz Taylor always marries the men she loves, and only yesterday I read one called: "Is Doris Day really the home-spun girl she appears to be?"'

'I bought this dress because I thought you'd like it,

146

when all the time I would really like to be sitting here opposite you wearing a glittering waistcoat over tweed plus-fours. So now you know.'

Only the appearance of the waiter stopped me revealing further truths about myself, and I was startled to see that Mark was laughing so much, he could hardly compose himself enough to give our order.

'So now you know,' I said again, as soon as we were alone, 'and unless you believe that opposites can be happy together, then there's no hope for us. But I do love you,' I added.

When you're twenty-five and you've been in love four times, and each time it's come to nothing, and this time you know that if you're let down again there's nothing for it but a cat, and parcels of fish in your drawer at the office, the future can look very bleak indeed.

So bleak that you're not to be blamed if a tear escapes from your eye, and starts to roll down your cheek.

Then Mark leaned across the table, and with his forefinger gently traced the tear, and lovingly drew in the outline of my trembling mouth.

'Tell me something, darling?' he whispered.

'I've said it all,' I said sadly.

'Is Doris Day really the home-spun girl she appears to be?'

And as we laughed together, I knew that I'd found myself at long last.

The Drama

Outside the lilac tree is tapping on the window, and
the air holds the first nip of autumn, and here we are
again, sitting in front of the television set waiting for
the play to begin. Me in the pool of light from the
standard lamp, pleasantly doing nothing. You with
your chair twisted round, so that your back is turned
ever so slightly towards me.

The boys are out. Tony at an after-church Youth
Club get-together, Stephen with Yvonne.

. . . I wonder is she really as empty and shallow as
I think she is, or am I just childishly prepared to dislike
on sight any girl my beloved elder son brings home?

Yes, here we are, you and I, twenty years married,
no longer young, but a long way from being old; and
there is the play about to begin . . .

You watch unperturbed as the opening scene shows
a man and woman lying in bed together. She is in her
petticoat. It is black, of course, and he is bare; at least
the part we can see is bare.

He is smoking a cigarette, and she lies back and
watches him through long-lashed half-closed eyes.

The camera moves back a little to show the iron
bedstead, the crumpled sheets, the muddled squalor of
the room. There is a photograph of an open-faced
young man on the bedside table. We are shown a close-
up of his guileless features, and he is not the man in
bed with his chest all bare.

We know, without being told, that he is the husband.

The woman gets out of bed and pulls wispy nylons
over her shapely legs. We are spared nothing as she

149

fastens her suspenders, and you, my faithful husband, a pillar of our local church, and respectably chartered as an accountant, remain as if glued to the TV set.

Now you bend your head to light your pipe, and I see the round, thin patch on top of your head, and I remember that once you looked as young and virile as the man in bed, who is now lighting another cigarette and telling the woman that their affair is 'all washed-up' – that nothing, not even love, lasts for ever.

She cries beautifully, with what must surely be real tears running from her eyes, and glistening like dew-drops on her cheeks. It is very clever of her to be able to cry so beautifully, and to order, like that, but the man isn't impressed. He is laughing now, and leaning back against the iron bedstead. His thick lips curl into a curve of cynicism as he draws deeply on his cigarette.

She is wiping the tears away on the back of her hand, and now her fingers curl round a beer bottle. I hope that it is empty, because it is perfectly obvious that she is going to throw it . . .

'The things they do in plays!' you say, and raise a quizzical eyebrow at me, and I blush a little.

Because it isn't only in plays that things are thrown. Oh, no! And yet now I can't remember the reason why I threw it. But I do remember that it was a cup of tea, half-way drunk and blessedly cool.

The man in the bed is smiling enigmatically, and wham! the bottle misses his head by a mere fraction of an inch, and smashes into smithereens against the wall. A tiny smile of creamy contentment lifts the corners of the woman's mouth, and I know *exactly* how she feels . . .

But only for a moment did *I* feel like that, the next minute I was all contrition, begging for forgiveness, and watching with horror as the dregs of tea spread themselves into a stain of incredible diameter on the newly papered wall behind your head.

You know something, darling? I honestly believe that stain was bewitched! Nothing would remove it completely, and it stayed there, an everlasting monument to my shame until you re-papered the room.

However, the woman in the play doesn't seem to be suffering from the slightest pang of conscience. Wham! there goes a vase, and the clock, and another bottle, and finally, when there is nothing left to throw, she takes off her shoes and throws those. Skilfully, and with what seems like long practice, her lover ducks out of the way, and nonchalantly buttons his shirt over his chest, whistling underneath his breath.

Suddenly a door bangs back, and there stands the husband, with his guileless features blurred into lines of disbelief. There is a sharp exchange of bitter words, and we learn without any surprise at all, that the man knotting his tie is the best friend he would have trusted with his life.

I sigh, and grope underneath a cushion for my knitting.

'Are there no plays about happily married couples?' I say, but you are leaning forward eagerly as the husband knocks his best friend clean through the doorway, and all the way down a dingy flight of stairs.

I start a purl row, and think about your best friend. I think about all the husbands of all our friends . . .

Am I abnormal because I have never been in the least in love with any of them? Is it stranger still, that not one of them has ever been in love with me?

The woman runs out into the night, a coat thrown over her disarray. I hope that she has remembered her shoes. It's raining, of course, and the streets are black and deserted, and the camera follows her down sordid alleyways, across a cobbled courtyard, and now and again we are shown a close-up of her white and strained expression.

Now outside our own window there is a soft flurry of rain, and I get up and draw the long yellow curtains, and switch on another bar of the electric fire.

The fight is over, and you have lost all interest in the play, and you lean back, your head lolling, your mouth open, and your chin folded over your collar.

I stand by your chair, and think what an unlovely sight you are, and how much, how very much I love you.

And now I remember why I threw the cup of tea at you. It was a long time ago, and our new television was only of the one-channel, nine-inch-screen variety: and yet you, who had said that television was the death of all civilised living, were held irrevocably in its spell. Even the test card held a fatal fascination for you . . .

I remember it just as if it were yesterday.

It had been one of 'those' days, Tony, for the third time had pinched crayons from school, and brought them home on his head cunningly concealed beneath his cap. Were we nurturing a kleptomaniac, I worried? And Stephen: was that swollen knee really a bone chipped in a rugger scrum, or indicative of something far more sinister? And how on earth had the red sock got into the washing machine and turned your best white shirt and underpants pink?

I wanted to talk to you, that was all, just to talk the tensions of my day away, but nothing could induce you to slew your eyes a fraction of an inch in my direction.

'Perhaps Tony needs psychiatric treatment,' I said, and 'Mm, mm, mm,' you said.

'Perhaps I can bleach it out,' I said.

'Shush, love,' you said . . .

You really deserved it, darling, but I quickly discovered that I wasn't a thrower at heart, and you've been quite safe since then.

On the television screen, out in the dark streets, the

woman is still running, exhausted, wet through, and almost demented.

I toast my knees by the fire, and feel sorry for her, and am humbly thankful that I have never had the urge to run out into the night after another man . . .

And when she finds her lover, what does he do? He pushes her away from him, and tells her again that they are 'all washed up.' Hysterically she sobs, and there in your chair, uncaring, you sleep on. I look at the clock and decide that it is almost time the boys were in, and that I will make the coffee.

I clatter the cups on to the tray because I want to see the end of the play, but I am just too late. The names of the cast are rotating neatly round the screen, and now I shall never know what happened to the sad-eyed desperate woman.

Gently I nudge you awake and hand you your cup of milky coffee. Your eyes blink up at me, daring me to say that you have been to sleep.

'What happened at the end?' I ask, and craftily you say that it was one of those endings that could be interpreted in many ways . . .

So here we sit, twenty years' married: no longer young, but a long way from being old, drinking our milky coffee and waiting for the boys to come in. We appear smugly old fashioned to them, and contentedly dull.

I reflect that in thousands and thousands of houses all over the country, all over the world, married couples will be doing the same; loving each other, exasperating each other, even mildly putting up with each other. Sharing moments of unreasoning anger interspersed with moments of unspeakable joy.

Nothing lasts for ever, the man in the play said, and oh, I think how wrong he is . . .

Some things last for ever, especially love.

Yes, especially love, my darling.

The Christening

He lay on his back, one arm round Laura.

At last, the noises in the house had died away. The ceiling had settled down from the rock 'n' roll session the Briggs family was having upstairs. The Jameses next door had given up screaming at each other and gone to bed.

Laura was fast asleep. Her breathing was deep and even, but now and again a fluttering sigh reminded him of the tears that had gone.

He couldn't get over that. There was this Lancashire bloke on the wireless telling corny stories in an accent so broad he could only tell one word in three. There was Laura putting his sandwiches up for the next day. Then, suddenly, without any warning, she was crying as if her heart would break. She had put her head down on her arms, and her hair had spread out over the rather dirty tablecloth.

And when he'd asked her why she was crying, Laura had said: 'Nothing, Bill, honest, it's nothing,' and then gone on making the sandwiches.

Women, he thought, and gave himself up to the soothing wave of sleep creeping over him. He tightened his hold on Laura.

All the same, he'd hated seeing her cry like that.

Then the baby started to cry. 'Blast, oh blast,' Bill said softly, and lay still, hardly daring to breathe.

Perhaps, if he didn't move, the little so-and-so would drop off again. But the whimper became a wail, and the wail a piercing yell.

Laura sat up, but he was out of bed first. He felt the

155

shock of cold green linoleum against his bare feet as he groped for the switch.

'Stay where you are, love, I'll get her,' he said.

The cot was over by the far wall, and inside it the baby was a wet bundle of screaming fury. Her eyes were slits in a round, crimson face, and when Bill picked her up he wrinkled his nose against the stinging smell of ammonia coming from the sodden nappy.

'Give her to me,' Laura said, 'and I'll change her while you get the bottle.'

Bill hitched his pyjama trousers tighter round his middle, and reached for the pan. A little warmth came from the flickering gas ring, and he held his frozen hands as near to the pan as he could.

The baby cried in hiccoughing, penetrating sobs, and soon the Jameses next door were knocking on the thin dividing wall.

'All right, all right,' Bill shouted, testing the bottle expertly on the back of his hand. 'We 'eard you the first time.'

Back in bed it was all right again. Bill snuggled down underneath the clothes and put his head against Laura's side and squinted up at her, watching her feed the baby. Her fair hair fell forward over her pale cheek, and the tip of her tongue protruded slightly as she concentrated on holding the bottle at exactly the right angle.

'I love you,' he said slowly. 'Tell me why you cried tonight.'

'It was nothing,' she said, holding the baby against her thin shoulder, and patting it with small, comforting caresses.

'Tell me why you cried,' he said again.

The baby was gulping greedily once more before she spoke. 'It was that man on the wireless. He – he reminded me of my dad like. His accent, you know?'

Bill jerked away from her, and lay on his side staring at the damp patch on the far wall.

'You promised me, we wouldn't never mention them no more,' he said at last.

Laura got out of bed, and he heard her settling the baby down again. She snuggled up to his back, and put her thin arm round him. He held his breath as he heard her voice tremble on the verge of lost control.

'But they're my mum and dad, don't you see?' she said.

Bill wanted to stroke the cold bare arm lying uncomfortably across his chest, but he held himself stiffly aloof. Now Laura was crying again, and her body was shaking with deep sobs.

'You never had a mum and dad, so you don't see,' she choked.

'You'll wake the baby,' Bill said, but he clenched his fist to stop himself from turning round to comfort her.

'You never said you was homesick,' he said. 'You said you liked Birmingham. You said you never wanted to see them again after the things they said.'

Laura whispered fiercely against his back. 'They was mad, because of the baby, and because it couldn't be a proper wedding or anything.'

Oh, the wedding! Bill thought. The Methodist Chapel, cold and bare at nine o'clock on a Saturday morning. No flowers, no organ music, no guests in fancy pink hats. Just the solemn voice of the old minister, and Laura's mother sniffing in the front pew, and Laura white-faced and unfamiliar in a new blue coat and hat.

That time in the chapel, saying those words after the minister, was the only time he had felt ashamed of his love for Laura. And her mum and dad had done that for him. What else could he do but bring her right away from them? At least her mum could hold her head up with them out of the way.

*

Bill turned round and gathered Laura close to him. He tangled his fingers in her hair, and kissed her tears with gentle, husbandly persuasiveness.

'If they could just see the baby,' she said. 'If they could just' – her voice faltered – 'If they could just come to the christening.'

Bill sighed. He saw Laura's mum, small and prim, with her dark hair scraped back and her mouth buttoned up, tight and prissy. He saw her beady glance take in the cracked wash basin, the faded wallpaper, the cooker out on the landing, and the bed sagging in the middle like a loose tarpaulin.

'It's not what our Laura's been used to,' she'd say.

And her dad, who alone, was like the hearty comedian on the wireless, but who changed into a silent non-entity when his wife was there. How he had hated them both.

But he held Laura close and murmured into the softness of her hair. 'All right, love, they can come if you want it that way.' After all, she was a long way from home, and only sixteen.

'Bill, oh Bill,' she whispered and covered his face with quick eager kisses.

Women, he thought again from the depths of his seventeen-year-old wisdom. They knew how to get their own way all right.

To Love and Let Go

My daughter's name is Jane. She has always been small for her age, and now that she is twenty-eight, she still looks about seventeen. But then, don't all modern girls with long straight hair worn with a fringe, who seem to live in jeans and sloppy sweaters, with hips no wider than a hand-span, still look seventeen?

She is married to a serious, kind young man who is doing well in a bank, and she has three children, all girls, and the eldest is only six years old, and last night we talked on the telephone as we do once a week, and she told me that she had a 'kind of flu'.

'Not badly,' she said. 'Honestly, Mummy, not badly,' but even with two hundred miles separating us, her voice had that washed-out sound to it, and I knew that she ought to be in bed with a hot-water bottle, and soothing blackcurrant drinks, but I didn't say so, because as she would have said, how can a mother of three little girls go to bed with something as innocuous as a feverish cold?

If I lived nearer, I would go to see her this morning. I would catch the bus out to the new estate where she lives near London, where every house is exactly like its neighbour, right down to the last grain of pebble-dash.

Although my daughter is small, she is healthy and strong, but when she has a cold, she has a temperature; her eyes run, her nose runs, and she is diminished. Yes, that is the word. She is diminished. Her colds always leave her with a sore throat, and when she was a child I would put her straight to bed, and minister to her.

Hot drinks, lozenges, her favourite books on hand,

and the radio turned low, and until she was in her scornful teens, her beloved teddy-bear tucked in beside her for company.

Even then, right up to the time she got married at nineteen, her colds were always of the extra virulent variety.

I remember how she had a dreadful one the week before the wedding, and how she wailed that she would be going down the aisle in her white dress, red of eye, snuffling as she made her responses, and how the very thought of such a catastrophe made her temperature rise, and how I got up in the middle of the night, and brought her hot lemon and aspirins, and promised her on my own life that she would be better on the day.

I remember the jellies I made to soothe her poor throat, and the egg custards she scorned, and I recall the way I would sit with her, just being there, believing as I do, that love is the best medicine of all.

But now she is a wife, and a mother of three, and all I can do is sit in my too-tidy house, two hundred miles away, and imagine just how it will be.

I can see her clearly, lank of hair, blue eyes shadowed with weariness, and the tip of her small nose a fiery pink colour.

She was perfectly all right, she assured me last night, her voice hoarse with the effort of assuring me that she is all right, but in my mind's eye I see a massive pile of ironing, and my fingers itch to work on it, and the knowledge that she has been down in the garden hanging them out in this cold east wind makes my own bones ache in sympathy.

The baby, eighteen months old – the one who was going to be a boy – has hands like the knuckle end of hams, which twitch when she isn't busy dismantling something that was never made to be dismantled. She climbs on everything, including the draining board, and I imagine her pulling herself on to a chair, balancing precariously on the arm, reaching for an object put on top of the bookcase out of harm's way, and I see my daughter, wanting to smack her, but too tired to smack her, wanting nothing more than to put her head back, close her eyes and have a few minutes' sleep.

I make myself a cup of coffee, and as I drink it, I see the two elder girls coming in from school, and I see them in their school uniforms, their blouses whiter than white, and know that Jane, who used to leave her own clothes in a heap on the bedroom floor, confident that they would be washed and ironed and hung in her cupboard the next time she saw them, would have got up that morning, pale and snuffling, seeing them off to school with a cooked breakfast, because that's the way she is.

If only I could be there, I would boil two eggs for their tea, and they would grumble – one because her egg is too soft, and the other on account of her egg being too hard. I love them dearly, but I would try to explain to them that their mother isn't feeling too well, and that they must help her and be good girls, and I can see the expression in their round eyes as they would stare at me, their nannie, whom they like because I bring them sweets which are normally forbidden, and read Paddington Bear to them. But I doubt if they would understand.

I would leave them grumbling over their toast fingers, and I would go upstairs to the bathroom, and the baby would be 'swimming' in the bath, vigorously as any cross-Channel swimmer. And I hear my daughter telling me again, as she did on my last visit, that she doesn't think her youngest one will ever be potty-trained; that she seems to *like* being dirty, smelly and messy, and I see the soiled nappy, and the pile of little clothes – the vest and dungarees, and the pink sweater,

161

egg-trimmed – and I stare out of my own window, and see my own day's washing hanging there, one nylon shirt, one pair of panties, one bra and a pair of socks, and I feel so helpless I could cry.

The baby will not be touched by anyone but her mother and father, not even by me, and she is large of build, and as heavy as a massive sack of potatoes, and twice as uncooperative, and Jane will have to lift the squirming bundle out of the bath, and in all probability chase the bare-bottomed little figure down the landing when she runs away.

And I know that the two downstairs, lying flat on the sitting-room carpet watching television, still have to be bathed, and that, when at last they're tucked up in bed, their mother will have to prepare an evening meal for her husband, and I guess that she will be too exhausted to eat anything herself.

I must add that I am not one of those middle-aged mothers who, when their family leave home, are left with time on their hands, to brood themselves into menopausal neurotics because they have nothing to do.

I work four afternoons a week at the local hospital as a library lady, and the ingredients for a casserole are neatly set out on the kitchen table, and before I leave the house the oven will be set to switch itself on at the appropriate hour.

I scrape a carrot, and find myself wishing madly and quite illogically, that I could parcel it all up and post its vitaminised contents down to Middlesex.

I must add also that we, my husband and I, gave our daughter willingly and happily into the care of her young husband on her wedding day. She is his responsibility now, and I know he will never shirk those responsibilities, because he is kind and loving, and rightly would not tolerate an interfering mother-in-law.

Mothers are supposed to cry on the day their daugh-

ters marry, but it wasn't like that with me. Oh no . . .
I was too busy praying to have time to cry, and my
prayer was: 'Make me into a good mother-in-law,
please God, because I have seen what a bad one can
do to a marriage. Amen.'

But being a mother-in-law doesn't stop me from
being a mother, and although I firmly severed the
emotional umbilical cord that day, I cannot stop myself
from wanting to run to my child when she is ill, even
though she is a child no longer.

I finish the casserole, and put it on the middle shelf,
then I go upstairs and get ready to go to the hospital
where the library books on their trolleys are waiting
for me.

I stare at myself in the mirror, and I tell my worried
face that I am every kind of fool, and my reflection
stares back at me . . . disbelieving, and not in the very
least impressed.

Love Is Like That

I knew the minute Jill came into the bedroom that she had been crying, so I lay still and pretended to be asleep. After all, there are moments in a person's life when she doesn't want to talk, even to her sister who is longing to know what is wrong, and could perhaps give her some good advice.

Jill had given up her room for Mother to use as a study. Mother was writing a novel, a hospital romance, because my father is a doctor and can supply the medical details. We were used to hearing her shout over the banisters, 'Darling, is it possible for a patient to propose to a nurse during a blood transfusion?'

'Have my room, Mummy. The view over the Green Belt will inspire you,' Jill had said. Just like that. She has just about the kindest heart in the world.

And now she was crying . . .

I could see she had got into bed without taking off her make-up, so I knew something pretty desperate had happened.

She gave a smothered sob into her pillow, and I couldn't stand it any longer. 'Had a good time at the party?' I said, which was a stupid thing to say to someone whose heart was obviously breaking.

'Oh, the party . . .' she said. 'We didn't stay to the end. We came away at eleven o'clock.'

I glanced at the illuminated face of the clock on the table between our beds. It said five minutes to twelve.

'Did you go back to Mark's flat?' I whispered, because I knew that Jill did that sometimes, although Daddy didn't like it because of what people might think. But as Jill is quite old, nearly twenty-one, she must be allowed to lead her own life, and if she doesn't know the difference between right and wrong now she never will, as Mother says.

'No, we didn't go back to the flat, we just sat and talked,' she said wearily. Then her breath caught on a sob, 'It's all finished. You might as well be the first to know, Amanda.'

I lay quite still; I felt as though I'd been dealt a mortal blow.

My sister Jill had had hundreds of boyfriends. Well, six at least, but not one of them compared with Mark in any way. He had simply everything, and then some to spare. Good looks – a sort of dark version of Doctor Kildare; black hair that looked fabulous, especially when it needed cutting; lots and lots of money, and a white shiny car with leopard-skin covers on the seats.

He hadn't asked Jill to marry him, but he was only biding his time, as Mother said.

I was counting on being their bridesmaid, and I had planned my clothes down to the last frill on my petticoat.

Blue, I had decided, the same deep blue as my eyes, with a cornflower worn flat on the top of my head; I am terribly tall and wouldn't want to tower over the best man, or anything sordid like that.

'Did you quarrel?' I asked, because as anyone knows, lovers quarrel all the time.

I mean to say, Tim and I fought regularly, and yet we had been going together for six whole months and one and a half weeks. Since my fifteenth birthday, in fact.

Jill was taking a long time to answer, and when she spoke her voice was funny, just as though she had learnt what she was saying by heart.

I switched on the bedside lamp and raised myself on one elbow.

My goodness, but she had been crying all right. Her

eyes were puffy and her mascara had run in black rivers down her cheeks, and her dark hair had come unpleated at the back, and hung down over one shoulder. She looked terrible!

Her face was stiff with hurt, and I switched the light off again, and lay down.

Jill sniffed into her pillow.

'He's found someone else. A model. Her name is Lucinda, and she has red hair and speaks Russian. They met at a cocktail party last week.'

'The party you missed because you had promised to watch me in the school play?'

Jill choked, and I lay there thinking.

I had known that Jill didn't really want to go to that play but I had walked about looking hurt for days because she said she couldn't go.

I was the Snow Queen, and my costume was so delicate, so filmy, that my friend Kathy, who writes soppy poetry, said it seemed to be made of moonbeams.

With my fair hair curled up at the ends I looked absolutely fabulous. And that's not being conceited; it happens to be true.

I wanted all my family sitting there in the middle of the front row, clapping like mad, and while they were doing just that Mark had gone to the cocktail party alone, and met this red-haired Lucinda.

'Goodnight, Amanda,' Jill said, and I knew that she was going to lie awake all night, staring into the darkness.

And it was all my fault!

I wanted to jump out of bed and throw my arms round Jill, and say how sorry I was, but you're either that sort of a person, or you aren't.

So all I said was, 'Goodnight, Jill. Don't worry, it will work out.'

'Things do, don't they?' she agreed in that funny choking voice.

'Yes,' I said firmly, and we both lay there, engrossed in our thoughts.

Then I dreamt that I saw Mark standing outside a church. He was shabby and almost unrecognisable behind a big black beard. The church door opened, the organ music pealed out, and Jill appeared, wearing a fabulous white dress, and veil.

The man looking down into her eyes was a cross between Bronco and Mike Sarne. As they came out into the sunlight, Mark walked away sadly, his head bent, and his feet, in scuffed shoes, shuffling through the dust.

'There's more fish in the sea than ever came out of it,' Father said at breakfast.

'Time is a great healer,' said my mother, taking the third piece of burnt toast from underneath the grill.

Jill sat there, chewing and swallowing automatically, and now and again smiling briefly at us all. When she had left for work my mother angrily clattered the breakfast things together.

'I always knew that young man was a philanderer. His eyes were too close.'

I stared at her in astonishment. Every time Mark had called for Jill, Mother had behaved as though he was visiting royalty. She had done everything but roll a red carpet down the hall.

Tim walked home with me from school. I wasn't allowed to go out with him; my parents are very old-fashioned and stipulate no dates until I am sixteen. Imagine!

It didn't really matter, because they also believed in encouraging me to bring friends home, so Tim had more or less moved in with us!

We put a pile of records on as soon as we got into the house, and the very first song was a haunting piece about someone losing their only love. There were soaring violins and the words were so sad I started to think about Jill again.

Tim can be very understanding for a boy, so I told him all about it.

'So you see, it was my fault. I was nothing but a selfish beast.'

Tim nodded. 'Yes you were, and it was your fault,' he agreed at once.

Well, it is one thing to call yourself a selfish beast, and another thing to have someone agree with you. Especially someone who is supposed to be your friend! So within two minutes flat, Timothy Barnes was being shown out of the front door in a silence dripping with dignity.

My mother's tousled head appeared over the banisters.

'Tim gone? Put the potatoes on, darling, will you?' she said.

My thoughts as I turned on the gas under the pan were very bitter. How could my own mother write such thrilling romances, and yet be unaware of the heartbreak going on in her own house?

I sprinkled salt on the potatoes, then threw some over my left shoulder for luck. Not that it would do any good.

And it didn't. The next day Tim walked home with Sandra Mayhew, who has worn tight skirts and lipstick since she was twelve.

Jilted, like Jill. Thrown aside like a worn-out glove. A pair of worn-out gloves . . .

I missed Tim terribly, but I didn't burden anyone with my troubles, even Jill; she was having enough trouble of her own.

In one short week she seemed to have gone painfully thin, all shadows and hollows. She was only going through the motions of living. Anyone could see that.

Then she would sit on the edge of the bed, staring at the space where Mark's photograph used to be, her brown eyes misty with unshed tears.

She was sitting like that, pretending to watch television, the following Saturday evening, when the telephone rang. It was about the time Mark usually rang to say what time he would pick her up.

Jill jumped a mile, a deep blush staining her cheeks, hope reflected in her eyes.

'Oh, please let it be Mark,' I prayed as I went into the hall. 'Please, please let it be Mark.'

'Amanda?' said Tim's voice.

I was so surprised and glad, and yet so furious with him for not being Mark, that I slammed down the receiver. Then, ashamed of myself, I went slowly back to the living room.

Jill had slumped down in her chair.

'Wrong number,' I mumbled, and she nodded, and pretended to be interested in a little man balancing a stick with a ball on the end of it on his nose on television.

He was balancing the same stick with a ball on the end of it on his feet, when the telephone rang again.

This time my mother put down her pencil and went into the hall.

'If it's Tim, I'm out,' I said, and she came back looking most aggrieved.

'Children shouldn't encourage their parents to tell lies,' she said. 'When I was your age . . .'

I spoke quickly. 'It's marvellous, Mummy, the way you can write with the television on, and us talking.'

Immediately, at the mention of the word writing, she forgot what she had been going to say. She beamed at me.

'Jane Austen did it all the time, darling,' she said. 'She could prop her notebook on the mantelpiece, and write away, in a room crowded with people. Nothing disturbed her once she had got into the flow.'

'A sign of true genius,' I agreed.

But when we were undressing for bed that night, Jill spoke through the folds of her nylon nightdress.

'I don't know how you could treat Tim like that. If – if anyone I was fond of rang me up, I wouldn't be able to stop myself telling him how much I'd missed him – that would be if he . . .'

Her voice tailed off miserably, she got into bed and switched off the light.

I finished putting my rollers in by guesswork, and lay down.

Yes, I thought. That's exactly what you would do. You'd run and run, straight into Mark's arms. That's what you've always done. You loved him so much, you were always there, ready and waiting for him. You would let him change his mind about your plans, and he'd know you wouldn't protest because you felt that wherever you went was all right as long as you were together.

I moved my head gingerly on the pillow. My head felt as though I were wearing a crash helmet, and I was thankful that I usually wore my hair straight, but I had to persevere. If I knew Tim, he would be round the next morning, and I wanted to look my best when I finally forgave him.

The next morning I got up at least an hour earlier than usual, and put on a dress instead of my usual Sunday morning jeans and sweater. I peeled the potatoes in a frilly hostess apron, and tried to make my mother see my point of view about Jill.

'She ought to have played more hard-to-get,' I finished. 'That's what I think.'

'Try not to use vulgar expressions, dear,' Mother said. 'We are all as God made us, you know.'

171

Her eyes, as she basted the joint, were glazed, and I knew that she was busy hatching up another plot.

'But surely you see . . .' I was beginning to say, when the door bell rang.

It was Tim, just as I had known it would be.

He stood there on the doorstep, wearing his blue jeans, and a yellow pullover.

'I was just passing,' he mumbled, and fascinated, I watched a blush creeping over his freckles. 'I was just passing and I wondered if you . . . that is . . .'

Throwing aside my apron, I opened the door wide, gave him a gracious smile and invited him in. We went into the sitting-room, and put a record on, and it was just like old times.

When Jill had drifted in and out for a moment, all pale and wan, I couldn't resist getting Tim to confirm what I already knew to be the truth.

'Were you furious when I wouldn't speak to you on the telephone last night?' I asked him out straight.

'Furious? That isn't the word. That's why I've come round. To see what is going on . . .'

That was all I wanted to know.

When Tim went an hour later he had promised to help me with my physics homework. I watched from the window as he ran up the road and I should have been happy, yet I wasn't. How could I be happy when Jill spent all her evenings by the telephone waiting for it to ring, and all her nights crying into the darkness for Mark.

'You will have to pull yourself together, Jill,' my mother said. 'No man is worth so many tears.' And she gazed fondly at my father and passed him another piece of his favourite cherry cake.

'There's more fish in the sea than ever came out,' my father began when the telephone rang, and once again I saw hope in Jill's eyes, only to die when the caller turned out to be the butcher in the high street, whose wife was having her fourth baby.

I knew something would have to be done, and quickly, or my sister would become a nun, or a missionary, or something drastic like that.

So I spent three of my lunch hours cycling to and fro in front of the restaurant where Mark usually had lunch.

And I was just about to give up, when on the third day I saw the shiny white car parked outside. I managed to fall off my bicycle just as Mark came out through the swing doors.

He rushed to pick me up, as I had planned he would, and when I looked up into his face I could almost understand why Jill was breaking her heart for him. His eyes were hazel, with little flecks of green in them, and his hair sprang away from his forehead in crisp dark waves.

I smiled shakily and limped over to my bicycle.

'I'm all right, really I am,' I said. Then I staggered in a realistic way – I hadn't been chosen to play the Snow Queen for nothing – and put my hand to my head.

'Just a little dizzy for a moment,' I said bravely, and sort of slumped over.

Swiftly Mark wheeled the bicycle to the kerb, propped it up, opened the car door and deposited me on one of the leopard-skin seats.

'I will run you back to school and someone can collect your bicycle later,' he said.

I swallowed hard as he let in the clutch. That wasn't in my plan at all.

'Please, no,' I gasped. 'I shouldn't be out of school really. Just let me sit here for a few minutes until the shock has worn off, then I'll wheel my bicycle back myself. I won't ride it, I promise.'

I managed a sort of watery smile, and he took out his handkerchief, and wiped a streak of mud from my face. Mark was just about the nicest person I had ever known. I forgot that I was supposed to be in a state of shock and smiled at him.

He grinned back, then suddenly was serious; 'And how's Jill?' he said.

'Dying of a broken heart,' I wanted to say, but I remembered my plan.

'Oh, she's fine,' I said. 'Not that I see much of her. She goes out nearly every evening, and when she comes in, I'm asleep.'

'Out?' he said slowly. 'Nearly every evening?'

'Yes, you know, parties, dances and things.'

He rubbed his chin thoughtfully.

'That doesn't sound like Jill.'

'No, it just goes to show, doesn't it?' I said, and watched him frown and beat a worried tattoo on the steering wheel.

I started to fumble with the catch of the door, and he leant across and opened it for me.

''Bye Mark, and thank you,' I said. He didn't speak, and when I walked away I knew that he was still sitting there with that puzzled look in his eyes.

We had English literature that afternoon and Miss Arkwright, who has fawn-coloured hair, read us a long poem about love. She read it with deep feeling, and a catch in her plum-in-the-throat voice.

Poor Miss Arkwright. Was that how Jill would look in about twenty years' time? And would a poem be all she had left to remind her of a love that might have been?

I felt pleasantly sad for the rest of the day, and that evening the sky was a faded blue and the lilac bush by the front gate drooped low with scented blossoms.

I leant out of the window, just in time to see Mark's car slide to a stop. I was so surprised, I could hardly move. My plan had worked far quicker than I had ever dreamt that it would.

Mark was getting out of the car and looking towards the house. He hesitated, and I could have felt sorry for him if I hadn't remembered that he had broken Jill's heart.

Jill! She must be warned. I started to run downstairs. Whatever happened she mustn't let him know that she was glad to see him again.

'Jill,' I called, but it was too late.

She had seen the car from the living-room window and had rushed into the hall, flung open the front door, and then she was running, running down the path. It was a long path and her high heels made a clicking sound on the paving.

Slowly I walked back upstairs into my mother's study, and looked through the window. There was Jill, dark hair flying, skirts billowing, arms stretched wide.

'Don't let him see that you care so much,' I wanted to shout. 'Make him run to *you*!'

I hadn't realised that I was speaking aloud, until my mother came over to me.

'She's spoiling everything,' I wailed. 'Just look at her . . .'

My mother looked, then smiled at me and ruffled my hair.

'In every love affair there is one who loves the most. One who is quick to forgive, and for Jill it will always be like that . . .'

'But he hurt her so,' I said. 'And now she is asking to be hurt again. She should have made him think that she didn't care.'

But now Mark was holding Jill close in his arms and kissing her, a kiss that seemed to go on for ever. Then they walked together up the path, and waved to me, and their faces were full of joy.

Still I argued. 'She should have made him run to *her*.'

My mother shook her head.

'Some day you'll love like that, Amanda. Some day you'll understand that a woman can love without reservation. Be hurt, and still keep on loving. Give her whole heart and ask for nothing in return.'

She put the cover over her typewriter and went downstairs, leaving me alone.

I leant my forehead against the cool glass. Outside, the shadows were lengthening, and the birds in the eaves sang full-throated lullabies. The long summer evening was coming to a close.

'Some day you'll love like that, Amanda . . .'

Oh, never, never – I vowed to myself. I'll always be me, just like I am now. Belonging to nobody . . .

And yet, as I made my vow, the darkness crept into the room, and at the gate, the lilac blossoms drooped their heavy heads against an almost navy blue sky.

I cried, not knowing what I was crying for, until I felt empty, and drained, and beautifully sad. Then, just as I thought I would never stop crying, I suddenly remembered Jill would marry Mark, and I would be their bridesmaid.

In blue, I decided, to match my eyes, and with a flat delicate flower on top of my head, because I was tall, and didn't want to tower over the best man.

I leant out of the window, and felt the air cool on my face. Mother called up from the hall. 'Amanda, come down. Jill and Mark have something exciting to tell you.'

And with blue shoes to match, I thought happily, as I ran downstairs. I'd look fabulous.

Skip the Fish Course for Me

Deciding that I wouldn't see Jonathan again should have been easy. He wasn't the only pebble on the beach, as my mother was always saying. But there was a complication: I was hopelessly in love with him.

That Monday morning, I was slapping cleansing cream on Mrs Hadley-James's face in preparation for her weekly facial.

'Had a lovely weekend, Clare?' she asked. I replied that if sailing round the Isle of Wight in a freezing mist could be called a good time, I supposed I could say that I had.

'Your young man is as fond of his boat as ever, then,' she said. 'I understand. With mine used to be cricket until he got too old to totter out to the wicket. But I always used to comfort myself with the thought that he could have been obsessed with chorus girls and sex.'

I hoped my smile wasn't reflected in the mirror as I imagined old Mr Hadley-James chasing sequinned belly dancers.

The previous year Jonathan had received a legacy from an aunt, enough money to buy us a house. But he had spent every penny on a thirty-foot cabin cruiser, moored at Lymington! At weekends he could pick me up at the salon and have us both aboard at a time when I would normally have been taking off my workaday smock and changing into something more decorative.

Now I found myself grabbing a pair of jeans from a locker and pulling a heavy sweater over my head, watching as he plotted our course on his charts, listening as he conferred with the coastguard on the radio and standing by while he refuelled at the quayside.

The boat is called Laughing Girl, but I didn't feel much like laughing as I dashed about in rope-soled plimsolls obeying instructions barked at me by a Jonathan who would have made Captain Bligh sound like a country curate.

I am not a jeans and sweater kind of girl. My skin never tans, my hair is long and floaty, and I wear rubber gloves to wash up a couple of coffee mugs. I come into my own in the warm gloom of a restaurant, holding hands across the table and fluttering my feathery eyelashes at a man sitting opposite.

Fluttering eyelashes does not go with a thick woollen cap pulled low over the eyebrows and a face smothered in moisturiser in an attempt to thwart the ravages of wind and sea spray.

Sometimes I felt that Jonathan wouldn't have noticed if I'd appeared on deck naked. All he seemed to worry about was whether the motor was throbbing at the right number of revs per minute and whether the mackerel were biting with sufficient enthusiasm.

Mrs Hadley-James's face was encrusted now with a face-pack so, leaving her to set, I went into the staff room and rehearsed what I was going to say to Jonathan the following Saturday. I would tell him, without emotion, that if all he wanted was a second mate, he might as well take his little brother along. I would remind him there were other fish in the sea.

'And I don't mean mackerel,' I would add.

Saturday was a beautiful day for sailing, with the wind in the right direction and the sea a limpid green. Jonathan looked fantastic in his blue denims and T-shirt, his hair glinting in the sunlight and his blue eyes alight with happiness.

I was driving, while he fixed up two fishing lines at the back of the boat.

'Right!' he said, coming up behind me and putting his arms round my waist. 'I've a feeling we'll be frying tonight.'

'I don't care if we don't catch a single fish,' I said.

He looked at me astonished. 'Well, there's nothing else for supper. I'm sure I told you to bring bread and cheese.' Before I had time to answer he yelled 'A bite!' and dashed back to the line. I tried not to wince as he twisted the hook from a mackerel's gaping mouth and bashed its head against the side of the pail before throwing it in.

He said excitedly: 'I think we must have sailed into a shoal. Hope your mother's got an empty shelf in her freezer.'

He was right. For the next few hours he was so busy that I didn't have time to deliver my carefully prepared speech of farewell.

In the end we were plastered with fish scales, but after I'd grilled four mackerel in the galley and sprinkled them with lemon juice, even I had to admit that they tasted superb.

'We'll go back to the same spot tomorrow,' Jonathan declared as we tied up at our mooring place.

This time I said what I had to say. 'I don't wish to take part in tomorrow's fishing orgy,' I snapped, 'nor do I wish to spend any more weekends dressed like this, smelling like this. Nor do I wish to marry you,' I added, trying to control the trembling of my voice.

Jonathan said: 'But you love me!' 'Did,' I corrected, 'and now, if you'll get out of here, I'll take off these filthy clothes and you can drive me home.'

For most of the way we maintained an icy silence; when he stopped the car he glanced back over his shoulder at the bags of fish reposing on the back seat.

179

'I don't suppose . . .' he inquired humbly.

'My mother is fed up with mackerel,' I said, and ran up the drive to the front door.

'I'll ring you,' he called, all trace of Captain Bligh gone from his voice.

'I'd rather you didn't,' I shouted back. Then I ran upstairs to tell the mirror in my room that I'd done the right thing.

The next week was awful. Jonathan took me at my word and didn't telephone, though Mrs Hadley-James swore that he would. 'He'll ring and say that you must sit down together and work something out. "Every *other* weekend," he'll say. "A compromise. It's the only way."'

The telephone did ring that evening, but it wasn't Jonathan.

'Remember me?' a deep voice said.

'If you'd elaborate . . .' I said.

'Stratford-upon-Avon, 1976,' the voice went on, and suddenly I remembered Charles Balfour, a beautiful man who wouldn't have heard the call of the sea if it had been broadcast from the top of the Eddystone lighthouse.

'I've just dropped over from Denmark,' he said. 'I looked in my little black book, and lo and behold, your name was the first that came to mind.'

'Because my surname begins with A?' I suggested. He laughed, and invited me out to dinner. Jonathan wouldn't have had the money to tip the waiter at the restaurant he chose.

'This is the real me,' I purred at the full-length mirror as I waited for Charles to arrive. I wore pale grey floating chiffon, the exact colour of my eyes, my hair as smooth as silk, curling up at the ends, and high-heeled sandals consisting of mere whispers of leather ribbons.

'You smell gorgeous,' Charles murmured, as he

helped me off with my black velvet jacket in the foyer of the restaurant.

'We'll skip the fish course, I think,' he said when the menus were placed before us.

'Yes, definitely skip the fish course for me,' I said with a vehemence that made him raise an eyebrow.

'What have you been doing since last we met?' he asked with a smile when the question of wine was settled to his satisfaction.

'Deep-sea fishing,' I said, 'in a smelly jumper and smellier jeans.' Charles told me there was a haunting sadness in my eyes which suggested that a lot of water had passed under my bridge since our last encounter.

Dolefully I said: 'An oceanful,' and spent the rest of that wildly expensive meal talking about Jonathan and his obsession with deep-sea fishing and Laughing Girl.

'A straight-forward case of love me, love my boat,' said Charles. 'You could always sink the blighter, couldn't you, sweetie?' His dark eyes twinkled at me over the top of the candle. 'You know, pull out the bung or something when you're not too far away from the shore.'

'I can't swim,' I told him.

The food was superb, the wine went to my head a little, and Charles gazed at me with flattering concentration, but I couldn't help remembering the mackerel butties I'd eaten with Jonathan, and the fish scales sticking to his fingers when he touched my face.

Later, when Charles kissed me goodnight, he whispered: 'It's no good, is it?'

'What's no good?' I asked stupidly.

'Me and you,' said Charles. 'Your Jonathan has been there between us every minute, and you know it.' As he turned away, he added: 'Be happy, my sweet.'

I knew he was right. 'Thank you,' I said, as he drove away.

Next week the summer came to an end. The rains came and the wind blew like a March gale. Still Jonathan didn't ring.

I had my pride, I kept telling myself. But pride is wasted when you're in love. So I rang his flat when I got back from the salon the following Saturday. I let the telephone ring and ring. But there was no answer. Outside, the clouds were so low they wrapped the tops of the trees like a grey blanket and the rain lashed down.

Jonathan couldn't have gone down to the boat, I told myself. Even his obsession with Laughing Girl wouldn't allow him to take her out on a day like this.

Then I remembered the sadness in his eyes when I had told him our relationship was over. I pictured him steering the boat out of the harbour, his blue eyes narrowed with suffering, the rain mingling with the tears running down his cheeks.

My mother sighed when I asked if I could borrow her Mini to drive down to Lymington. 'He'll probably grow a beard and decide to sail round the world after you're married,' she said, 'and my grandchildren will be able to climb rigging before they can crawl.'

'Motor boats don't have rigging,' I said but she was smiling and I realised that I must have tried her patience hard that week, moping round the house, one ear cocked for the telephone.

I found Jonathan messing about on the deck of his beloved boat, wearing yellow oilskins and a hideous sou'wester.

For a moment I had a mental picture of Charles, immaculate in his dark grey suit, white shirt and hand-made tie. Then I was in Jonathan's arms and he was covering my face with kisses.

Later, when we were snugly settled in the cabin with two steaming mugs of coffee, he said earnestly: 'Clare,

182

I know I haven't been fair to you. I've been thinking it over, and I decided that if you came back to me' – for a moment I thought he was going to say he would sell Laughing Girl – 'we'd spend only every *other* weekend aboard.'

A compromise, I thought, a lovely, selfless compromise, give and take, the perfect recipe for a perfect marriage.

'Every weekend is fine with me,' I said. 'You could be doing a lot worse than messing about in boats and catching mackerel.'

'Such as?' said Jonathan, raising the eyebrows I couldn't see under the atrocious sou'wester.

'Chorus girls and sex,' I said, and burst out laughing at his blank expression.

'That's my laughing girl,' said Jonathan, and took me in his arms again.

Hello You

After he rang her she put in a request for the rest of the day off, pleading urgent domestic reasons, and her immediate superior, an anonymous, beige-faced woman, agreed at once, asking no questions.

Seeing him again after one long year was too important an occasion to dress for in the cloakroom at the office. She didn't want him to see her at the end of a busy day spent in harassed competence, dealing with claims and counterclaims . . . So she spent the afternoon at the hairdressers, then had a warm, scented bath, followed by a half-hour session lying prone on her bed, her face encrusted with a face-pack.

Her make-up took a long time to apply; she experimented with face-shapers, a midnight blue mascara, instead of her usual brown. And she agonised over what to wear, deciding at last on her black theatre coat, worn over a champagne-coloured dress of heavy silk.

She took a taxi to his hotel, and the streets into Kensington were clogged with traffic. Young people, squashed together into ramshackle cars, middle-aged couples, the man fuming at the wheel, the woman beside him fur-stoled and crinkle-haired.

Already she was ten minutes late, and she could imagine him glancing at his watch, trying to curb his impatience. Her unpunctuality had always irritated him.

At last her taxi slowed down to turn right, swinging into the forecourt of the fashionable hotel, and he was there, standing on the steps. He hadn't changed at all. He was just as tall, just as thin as she remembered, with that air of easy affluence about him which had made her so proud to be seen with him.

She saw him before he saw her. He looked anxious, and thinking of his anxiety on her account, the old, almost forgotten wave of tenderness engulfed her.

How was it possible, she asked herself, to love someone for a whole year, when even his letters, written from remote corners of the world, had dwindled to a few hastily scribbled postcards in the past few months?

What would he think if she told him that not one day had passed without her thoughts of him stilling her hand, or clouding her eyes with memories?

He saw her then, and came towards her, pleasure lighting his thin features.

'Hi, you,' he said, and for a moment she felt the butterfly touch of his mouth on her cheek. 'How lovely to see you. You're prettier than ever.'

'Hello, you,' she said. They smiled at the well-remembered greeting, but for her, already, the anguish had started.

One night, he had told her when he phoned. One night in London, before flying on to Cairo, or was it Rome? She honestly couldn't remember now.

He smiled at her. 'There's a drink upstairs. I haven't booked our table until nine,' and with his hand firm beneath her elbow, he walked her across the thickly carpeted foyer to the lift, chatting quietly.

How like him, she thought, to have booked a suite for just the one night, a suite with a balcony leading from his sitting-room. A balcony open to the late summer sky, and the muted hum of traffic far below.

'Brandy and ginger?' he asked, after he'd taken her coat, and she was pleased out of all proportion because he'd remembered her drink.

'And scotch on the rocks for you?' she said, in a fair imitation of his American accent. They laughed, and she felt young and gay and witty, the way she'd always felt when he was near to her like this.

'Tell me about you,' he said. 'When I rang your office, I was expecting them to say you'd gone away. In your last letter you mentioned applying for a transfer to Geneva. What happened to Geneva, then?'

'I changed my mind,' she lied, because it would have been quite impossible to tell him the truth; that after his last, scrappy postcard her hurt pride had made her write him a letter telling him she was going away.

It wasn't true; all the time she had stayed on in her flat letting chances pass her by, taking the Underground to Westminster each day to her job in one of the Ministries in Whitehall.

If he wanted her, she had reasoned, she would be there, unchanged. It had seemed as simple as that.

He sat down opposite her, in a chair that seemed too small for his tall frame, turning his glass round and round in his hands, as though he had something on his mind.

'I couldn't bear the thought of spending my one night in London alone. And besides, I wanted to see you, honey. You've been on my mind. Especially these last few weeks.'

He seemed to be searching for words. 'You were just great writing me those letters, and I sure did appreciate them . . . even though my being on the move meant that it took some of them an awful long time to catch up with me.'

Suddenly, the bright gaiety was gone; she felt a sense of unease she couldn't define, and she started to twine a strand of her long hair round and round her finger, then checked herself and asked for a cigarette. Immediately he stood up and offered her one from an expensive-looking gold cigarette case that looked new.

187

As she took it, his fingers brushed against her own, and she felt the long-remembered shiver of pure delight.

Then, abruptly, her see-sawing emotions turned to anger and she drew fiercely on the cigarette, so that the lighted end glowed brightly in the fast-gathering darkness.

'I don't recall you smoking,' he said, and she made some remark about it being a habit she'd acquired since he went away.

A silence fell.

'How was the trip over?' she asked quickly, and as he told her about the long frustration of a three-hour delay in New York, and the man who'd snored beside him on the plane, she was half closing her eyes, seeing him through a haze of smoke.

How easy it was to remember with aching vividness their last night together, just twelve months previously, before he'd left to go home.

How was it possible, she thought, to sleep with a man for the first time – the only time – to lie all night long with his head on her shoulder, and then to talk like this across a room, inquiring about each other with the conventional politeness always expected of very casual acquaintances?

It was only after he'd gone she'd started to chain-smoke. When week after week she'd re-read his letters, searching for some sign that he was feeling the same way; that because of what they'd done, they were *committed*. That the physical expression of their love had changed him, as it had changed her. That life could never be the same again.

She had tried to tell him at the time, but he'd teased her, and told her that if she had one fault, one teeny small fault, it was that she was too intense.

Perhaps it was true; if loving a man so much that

one would willingly give up everything just to be near him was being too intense, then he was right.

And he must know how much she loved him – hadn't the fact that she had slept with him proved that?

He'd actually said, she recalled, that for a man it was different, biologically different, and bemused and half awake, she'd listened and it hadn't been hard to forget what he had said . . .

It was only now that she remembered them, with him sitting there opposite her, and she wondered what he'd say if she told him that for a whole year there had been no other man for her. She had been out on casual dates, of course, she was no recluse, and once she'd tried hard to fall in love, but it was no good.

A part of her, she hastily qualified that, the whole of her being had been waiting for a sign that he was coming back to her. She stirred uneasily. Perhaps that was different too, for a man. Perhaps he would think her actions silly and sentimental, the reaction of a foolish woman.

She saw him glance at his watch, and she spoke too quickly, embarrassment making her voice too high, as though the amber-coloured brandy had been her third and not her first.

'My last letter was returned, so I was glad when you telephoned. I thought perhaps you were ill, or had gone away . . . or something.' Her voice tailed away, and she saw with surprise that his easy nonchalance had changed to an embarrassment to match her own. He got up, walked over to the balcony windows, then came back to his chair again.

He said: 'I'm always going away. You know that, and then the firm moved down to Texas, so I've moved down there.'

'Yes?' she said, but her smile was an effort and her fingers tightened round the stem of the glass in her hand.

He ran his fingers through the crisp darkness of his black hair . . . 'Look, honey. Maybe it would have been better if I hadn't phoned you but I'm fond of you. I guess a part of me will always be fond of you and I'm not the kind of guy to . . . to . . .'

'To what?' she heard her voice say, faintly.

'Aw, hell, to just disappear, though God knows in my job that would have been easy enough. I mean with some girls there'd have been no problem, but you're different. I couldn't do that to you, you're too . . .'

'Intense?' the voice that didn't seem to belong to her said.

He came and sat beside her on the little sofa and instinctively she shrank away, but he took the glass from her and put it down on the table, then reached out to take her hands.

'I'm going to be married next month. To a girl I've known practically all my life . . . to tell the truth, that's the one reason I stopped off overnight. To tell you. I'm not the sort of guy who could . . .' He gave her hands a reassuring squeeze. 'You know how it is, don't you, honey? A lot can happen in a year.'

She smiled stiffly and as she congratulated him in a voice that didn't seem to be her own, she watched his eyes fill with unflattering relief.

The floor seemed to be dipping and swaying, undulating like the waves of a turbulent sea, and when he went to fetch her coat she closed her eyes and willed herself to be still.

He was right. A lot could happen in a year. Depending on so many things . . .

A lot. Or *nothing*. Sometimes nothing at all.

The Up-Thinker

David had known right from the beginning that Megan was not like other women. She was a vegetarian, a free-thinker; she had dabbled in spiritualism, toyed with the idea of becoming a Buddhist, was sure she had lived as a serving-maid in the seventeenth century, and once, overcome by emotion had given practically all her clothes to the wives of men serving long prison sentences.

Megan was as dark as David was fair; as short as he was tall.

David liked to read Tennyson because he explained that the poet could make words sing. He also liked to listen to music in the style of Tchaikovsky's 'Pathetique'. He said it made his heart soar to the stars and brought tears to his eyes.

Megan said that Tennyson was positively archaic, then she dismissed Tchaikovsky as an unmelodious moron . . .

She read Joyce, and the only kind of music that interested her at all was Jazz. Modern, of course.

On the face of things, being so entirely different, they ought not to have fallen in love at all. But one evening, walking home from a small cinema showing a Swedish film with sub-titles, they had stopped suddenly. David had traced with a finger the pure outline of Megan's throat, and kissed her on her surprised uplifted mouth.

The kiss that had started as a friendly gesture had left them both shaking, astonished and delighted at the passion it evoked.

Three months to the day after that kiss, they were married, and immediately Megan submerged herself into the role of David's wife, determined to play it to perfection. Single-minded to an obsessive degree, she ran her home with a meticulous attention to detail.

Then one day, browsing through a pile of second-hand books on a market stall. Megan had a find . . .

The book had a green cover and was written by an American Doctor of something or other. The first chapter was entitled 'Choose to be Sick or Choose to be Well'.

It explained quite clearly that bodily health was just a simple case of mind over matter . . .

Megan read bits of it aloud to David the same evening.

'No-one,' she explained earnestly, '*No-one* needs to be ill. All disease is a direct result of wrong thinking, wrong living, and a negative approach to life and its problems. Positive thinking is the greatest of all healers. Think *up*. Never *down*, and your body will repay you by glowing with perfect health.'

Her eyes shone, and her dark hair swung round her expressive face. David sighed as he realised she had found yet another cause to enthuse about, but because he loved her so much he listened patiently.

'It's symbolic me finding this book today, because, David my darling, I'm almost sure we're going to have a baby.'

David sat stone still for a moment. He was aware of sounds; the coal shifting in the grate, a car passing, the clock ticking away on the mantelpiece. Then he pulled Megan up into his arms, buried his face in the clean sweet smell of her hair, murmuring incoherent words of love.

All the poetry in his soul, all the tenderness in his heart, all his infinite love, reached out to her. He wanted to kneel at her feet, to encompass her with adoration.

There was nothing he wouldn't do for her. He would

take care of her, cherish her. She must rest, she must take every precaution to safeguard her health. He would make her put her feet up right now and he would go through and make her a cup of tea. He ruffled his hair until it stood up in a worried peak, and his broad forehead settled itself into wavy lines of acute anxiety.

Megan laughed out loud and stretched her hand out for the green book. 'Chapter Five. Quote!' she began.

'Having a baby is the most natural function in the world. It is the most exciting thing that can happen to a woman. It is the happiest time of all for her. Pain in childbirth is the direct result of over-civilising ourselves, the direct result of wrong thinking, the product of fear, learned very often from our mothers. It is ignorance personified . . . having a baby should be as simple as shelling a pea from its pod.'

David was very thoughtful as he filled the kettle.

He remembered the night his young brother Gareth had been born. They had tried to send him out of the house, but he was sixteen years old and not a child he had told them. So he had stayed in his room, muffling his ears against the frightening sounds.

And after it was all over they had allowed him to tiptoe in to see his mother.

At first he could hardly recognise her, lying there all pale and tired, with the aftermath of pain like a taut shadow on her usually serene expression. He shuddered, then reminded himself that his mother had been middle-aged whereas Megan was young and strong . . .

When he carried the tray through she was still reading the book.

'Morning sickness is a figment of an overworked imagination. The stomach is the sounding-board of the emotions. If we are bad tempered or upset, the stomach lining becomes red and inflamed. If we are anxious and full of fear the stomach lining grows pale and cold, and we are sick. Naturally!'

And so, in the early mornings, she would lie peacefully asleep, her tousled head on David's shoulder, her stomach lining blissfully normal.

He would try not to think of the nauseating, heaving void that passed for *his* stomach. He wasn't feeling angry with anyone, he wasn't feeling particularly upset or afraid. He was just feeling sick.

He had heard of course that such a thing could happen, especially when a husband and wife were very close. He supposed there was a kind of sympathetic telepathy between them.

But even as he thought it he dismissed the idea as ludicrous. It sounded just like one of Megan's outrageous theories – like a quotation from the green book.

As the months passed David found himself furtively consulting the well-thumbed pages. Megan looked fabulous. She was a living example of right thinking, and when she triumphantly entered the ninth month of her pregnancy, she told David that she would like him to be there at the birth.

'As a sort of silent cheer-leader,' she said.

David closed his eyes in case she could see the horror reflected in them . . .

Megan wanted her baby to be born at home, so he had of course known that he would probably be called upon to dash about carrying jugs of hot water, pacing worried paths round the kitchen floor. But to be an actual onlooker at what he firmly believed to be an exclusive feminine performance? His sensitive soul quailed, turned pale at the thought.

He promised to be there, but then took to worrying alone in brooding silences, even though, according to Chapter Thirteen, worry was an entirely wasted emotion. Megan told him so.

'Honestly,' she said, after one of her visits to the ante-natal clinic, 'the fuss some women make about a perfectly natural condition. Everyone there had heartburn, swollen ankles, middle of the night dyspepsia, middle of the afternoon exhaustion. All because of negative attitudes. Because they will give way to *down* thoughts.'

David stared with distaste at the green book lying on the coffee table. He measured the distance from the table to the fire and half stretched out a hand.

But what good would that do? There would be another book that convinced Megan that a baby could be brought up single-handed, that a *down*-thinking husband was a liability. There might even be a book somewhere that taught a baby how to have *up* thoughts – how to cry at the right time and be potty trained at three months old.

Megan patted him on the shoulder. 'You look tired, darling. Lean your head back and rest, the dinner's all organised. I'm just going into the bedroom to do half an hour's relaxation exercises before I make the gravy.'

'You've forgotten your book.' David scowled at the green cover.

She thanked him, giving him her all-embracing, well-adjusted smile. David closed his eyes and gave way to thoughts of the frankly *down* variety.

The next day he woke up with a headache, and in the evening as he let himself into the flat, the headache was still there, throbbing and insistent.

Usually Megan met him in the hall, but today her defiantly red maternity coat lay on the floor, obviously dropped there in a hurry.

Muffled sobbing noises came from the bedroom, and in there he found her lying across the bed, curled up in a disconsolate ball.

Swiftly he pulled her into his arms, rocking her backwards and forwards like a child, smoothing the tumbled hair away from her hot forehead, comforting her with whispered words of love.

'Tell me,' he pleaded. 'Whatever it is I'll make it come right again, but please don't cry like that.'

The tender words seemed to undo her. She sobbed as if her heart would break in two, so David held her closer still and wrapped the eiderdown round her.

'You must try and tell me, love.'

At last the words came . . .

'They've told me I can't have my baby normally. They say I have a small pelvis and have to have a Caesarean operation.' Her voice broke. 'All those exercises. All that relaxing, learning how to breathe. All that right thinking about the birth and now, just a prick on the back of my hand, then nothing, just *nothing*. I'm going to miss what the book says would be my happiest time of all. I'm going to miss woman's crowning achievement. I'm a failure, a hopeless, inadequate failure.'

David kissed her trembling mouth, tasted the saltiness of her tears. He knew that when he spoke he must say the right thing, must choose his words with special care.

'You aren't a failure, Megan,' he began. 'No-one is a law unto himself. There are times when everyone needs help, and now it seems that you are going to need help to give birth to our baby.'

He paused for a moment. 'The wonderful thing is when there *is* someone to turn to – like the surgeon who will perform your operation – and like me, a handy shoulder for you to cry on.' He grinned down at her. 'And now I'm going to make you the best omelette you've ever tasted.'

She managed a shaky laugh. 'Have you ever made one before?'

'There's always a first time for everything.' He kissed the tip of her nose.

She gave a shuddering sigh. 'Do you know what I could eat? What I would give my soul for a slice of?'

'Name it and you shall have it.'

'Beetroot,' she breathed, her swollen eyelids closing in ecstasy. 'Slices of red beetroot, floating in dark brown vinegar. I can see a dish of them all the time, but the book said that food fancies were the imaginings of a neurotic mind.'

David just smothered a loud laugh of relief. Megan, his lovely, talented feet-on-the-ground Megan – she was exactly like other women after all!

'Beetroot it shall be,' he promised, tiptoeing from the room.

'I don't think we have . . .' she began, her voice already thick with sleep.

But David didn't stop to listen.

Somehow, and from somewhere, he would produce a dish of vinegary beetroot for her supper. If he hurried he might just be in time . . . He opened the front door beaming like an idiot. Megan needed him, and *everyone* needs to be needed. Especially a father-to-be.

Seething with *up* thoughts, he set off at a brisk pace down the avenue en route for the shops.

The Power of Love

Michael reached for a cigarette, his third that day, although he had decided definitely to give up smoking. He drew in fierce, angry puffs.

Tessa was curled up in the window seat, her feet tucked underneath her, and her hands clenched together in her lap. Her small face was flushed, and her voice near to breaking.

'We ought to be grateful to Mummy and Daddy for letting us stay here. Some parents would have – the way things were – they would have . . . left us to fend for ourselves. And then what would we have done?'

Wearily, Michael stubbed the cigarette out in a fluted ashtray, then, from sheer force of habit, emptied it into the flowered wastepaper basket. He walked across the thick carpet and tried to take her into his arms. Childishly, she jerked away.

Fighting the despair that threatened to make him lose his temper, he tried to explain: 'Look at this room,' he began: 'There isn't a single thing in it that we've bought with our own money.' He kicked violently at an innocuous white nylon rug. 'With my teacher's salary, it would have taken weeks of saving to buy that alone. And that lamp.'

He fixed a beautiful peach-shaded lamp with a malevolent stare.

Tessa spoke quickly. 'But that was a wedding present. From Tante Odile.'

Michael sighed, and remembered Tante Odile. She had flown over specially from Paris for the wedding, and had worn black. Just as if it had been Tessa's funeral, not her wedding. Her stoutness had overflowed the narrow pew where she sat, and disapproval flowed from her all through the short ceremony. There had been no organ music, just the patient voice of the minister, saying the necessary words.

'It wasn't much of a wedding was it, love?' he said, touching her dark gold hair.

Tears brightened her blue eyes. It was the first time he had referred directly to the wedding. Obligingly he had played her family's game of pretending that everything was as it should be; that there had been no baby due to be born in an embarrassingly few months, and yet, even as he had made his vows, her mother's words had come back to him:

'How *could* you?' she had said, quite beside herself. 'We trusted you, we allowed you to take Tessa out. We never thought, never dreamed that anything like this would happen. Oh, I know it's happening all the time, but not to us. How can I face my friends? They're bound to know, to reckon up . . .'

He had had an hysterical momentary vision of the friends, fur-stoled, with elegantly waved heads bobbing, as they counted the months on plump fingers smothered in rings. That day, watching the flush of agitation staining her crêpe-ridged neck, he had felt ashamed. For the very first time he had regretted his love for Tessa, and the tangle it had got them into.

He held her close, and now she didn't move away, but snuggled into his arms, and relaxed like a kitten against him.

'I didn't mind about the wedding,' she said. 'It was Mummy who always used to talk about the kind of wedding I would have some day. She would stare at white flowing bridal gowns in shop windows, and smile to herself, and I'd know she was planning on how I'd look.'

Her eyes sparkled. 'And that was long before I met you,' she teased. 'Long before I met anyone, really. I

200

think Mummy had looked forward to my wedding day since the day I was born.'

Michael knew exactly how Tessa would have looked. Instead of the pale grey suit and pink frothy hat – it was the first time he remembered seeing her in a hat – she would have walked towards him in a mist of white drifting material.

Now he closed his eyes against the softness of her cheek, and gently turned her mouth round to his own. As they kissed he felt his very bones liquefy with tenderness.

'Oh, Tessa,' he said, 'I love you so. At least come and *look* at this house in Tavey Close. I've got the key in my pocket now, but I've got to return it to the agent tomorrow. We could afford the down payment. I've worked it all out carefully. There's a tiny garden where you could put the pram, and even if we only furnish one room at a time, it would be our own home. Tessa, we can't go on like this.'

She smothered his words with her kisses, and he marvelled again at how swiftly his tenderness could turn to passion. He must be lost in love for ever, when he could let all his dreams be so easily swept aside by the touch of the girl in his arms.

In the next room the baby began to cry, and Tessa pushed him gently away. Perversely he tightened his hold on her. 'Let him cry. He can't be hungry, you've just fed him. Besides, you're busy right now.'

But even as he kissed her, he sensed her withdrawal. In spirit she was already with the baby, comforting him with loving pats, and murmuring words of endearment into his round, bald head.

'Let him cry,' he said again.

Tessa twisted herself free. 'You know that Mummy always comes upstairs if we let him cry. There, I can hear her now.'

Michael opened the door to her as Tessa, in the next

room, lifted the baby from his nest of blue blankets. He smiled at his mother-in-law. His lips still tingled from Tessa's kisses, and he willed himself to make the smile a welcoming one. She nodded at him, and went to take the baby from Tessa.

'He's wet!' she accused, and went straight to the drawer where the clean nappies were kept.

She knew where *everything* was kept, Michael thought peevishly, and yet why shouldn't she? After all, it was her house.

Tessa was sitting in a low chair now, the baby balanced on her knee. She shook talcum powder over his pink bottom, heedless of the way it cascaded down the skirt of her dress. One tiny foot dangled helplessly from her knee, and Michael had a sudden urge to hold it in the hollow of his hand, to kneel down on the rug by Tessa, and to plead with her again.

But her mother was there, slipping the folded nappy underneath the baby, and holding the curved pin in her strong teeth. 'Shut the door, Michael,' she said, 'and switch on one bar of the electric fire. You'd be surprised at the amount of draught that comes through.'

Her voice was as loud as usual, trained by years of voicing her opinions to quaking committees. Obediently Michael closed the bedroom door, but first he went through it, and left them alone together.

Mother and only daughter. They had forgotten him already. Despondently, he sat down at a small table, and pulled a pile of exercise books towards him.

After only one year of teaching, he knew he had chosen the right career. He could feel the sympathy that flowed between him and the pupils as he stood in front of them. Discipline came naturally to him – he had no need to raise his voice, and already he could feel a kind of exasperated pity for poor Miss Anderson, with her flabby hands and hand-knitted boleros, who every day was terrorised by the teenage boys in the top form.

How she had blushed when the headmaster had announced at the morning prayers that the older forms were to have a lecture on sex by a visiting doctor.

Michael smiled to himself as he remembered the carefully casual expression on the face of the doctor as he bounded into the classroom, and drew his anatomical diagrams on the blackboard, then began his lecture.

At first, the girls giggled self-consciously behind their cupped hands; the boys sniggered, and stared anywhere but at the blackboard. But the doctor invested his lectures with the down-to-earth qualities of a human biology lesson. His explanations were clear, concise, and as impersonal as a page from a text book.

The questions put by the boys at the end of the lecture surprised Michael by their frankness. The whole complex business of sex had been neatly packaged for them, given its correct terms, and now they were prepared to discuss it freely. Then the doctor glanced at his watch, stopped the flow of questions, and dismissed the class.

Later, rubbing vigorously at the diagrams on the board, he said, over his tweed-clad shoulder: 'Some of the young blighters were taking the mickey out of me. I can always tell, but it pays to play dumb and answer them seriously.'

He blew the chalk dust from his fingers. 'Notice how the girls kept quiet? It's always the same. You never can tell what girls are thinking.'

'I would have thought it better to talk to them separately?' Michael said tentatively.

The doctor smiled a thin, superior smile. 'If you'll forgive me saying so, that's just where you're wrong. We believe that if sex is taught openly to both boys and girls, then they accept it naturally. It's all this previous concept of sex that's to blame for the sharp rise in illegitimacy. I expect you read in the press not long ago that one bride in eight was pregnant on her wedding day?'

Michael nodded, and tried desperately not to blush. 'No,' the doctor said decisively, 'show them openly exactly where promiscuous behaviour can lead them, and their natural intelligence will make the majority of them reject the obvious risks.'

And that, as far as he was concerned, was that, Michael thought wryly. Not once had the word love been mentioned; not once in the whole of the afternoon. But surely, that was what it was all about?

If only he had had the courage to keep the class behind after the doctor had gone. If only he had had the courage to stand there in front of them and say what he wanted to say; what he desperately wanted to say.

He might have stumbled a little in the telling, but the words would have come straight from his heart: 'All the facts you have just heard can't prepare you for what lies ahead.' Yes, that was how he would have begun.

Michael pushed his chair back and walked over to the window. A thin drift of drizzle spattered the pane.

'No words,' he would have told them, 'no diagrams can prepare you for the impact of love, for the sheer *power* of love. Real love, I mean, not infatuation. You can know in clinical and forthright detail how and under what circumstances a baby is conceived, but you can't know how true love can suddenly twist your heart, and make your emotions soar to the stars – can make you forget for just a moment of time all the well-taught facts of life.

'Love can sweep all your principles aside, all your firm beliefs, and destroy for you, and the one you love, everything that you hold sacred. Ephemeral desire cares nothing for the next day, or even the next hour. This is what you have to know. This is what you have to guard against with all your willpower . . .'

He jumped as the door opened behind him, and Tessa was there. She pushed a stray lock of hair from her forehead. 'He won't stop crying,' she said. 'Mummy says I'm mixing his feeds too strongly. But I'm sure that I'm not. The clinic says – '

Michael put his arms around her and held her close. 'Tessa, let me tell them we're grateful for the way they gave up part of their house to us. But we must stand on our own feet, we *must*, if we are to make things work out.'

Next door, the rhythmical sobs turned to loud, hic-coughing yells. Tessa moved away from him. She was near to breaking-point, he could see that, and yet he went on: 'Let me tell your mother about the house.'

She shook her head. 'We can't, not after the way they stood by us. They'll think we aren't happy here.'

Michael spoke quickly. 'Well, are we happy here, Tessa? We had a bad start, the baby coming when I was only just out of training college. Moving in with your family was the only thing we could do, but now . . .'

She bit her lip and frowned, then suddenly anger blazed from her eyes, making them incredibly blue. 'You should have thought of that before you . . . before you . . .' The voice, tight with resentment, was Tessa's, but the words were her mother's, and fury leapt like a flame between them. The baby's cries turned to pierc-ing screams, and all the shame of the past months, the humiliation, the guilt, and the remorse, culminated for Michael in a moment of wild, unreasoning anger.

'You weren't actually unwilling, were you?' he shouted. 'I had to marry you. They saw to that!'

The words hung suspended, and they stared at each

other, horrified, shocked and bewildered. If he had taken her in his arms and said that he was sorry, the words could have been unsaid, but her mother's firm footsteps crossed the room to the baby's cot.

Without a word, Tessa turned from him, and went out.

Michael stood still for a moment, his heart thudding violently against his ribs. Then he crossed to the table and, with a single sweep, knocked the pile of exercise books to the floor. As he ran down the stairs and through the hall he caught a glimpse of her father sitting, as usual, immobile before the television.

Heedless of the rain, he strode down the avenue, past the detached houses huddled in select isolation behind high privet hedges.

He had no clear idea of where he was going, and yet as he turned into the quiet cul-de-sac of small, rather shabby houses, he knew an inexplicable relief. He fumbled in his pocket for the key, and let himself into the empty house.

It was all as he had wanted to describe it to Tessa. The brown paintwork, the linoleum the exact colour of beef-tea, the sitting-room walls papered in the wrong shade of green. In the kitchen, the sink was cracked, and the draining board ingrained with dirt. How could he have expected Tessa to come here? And now, after what he had said, she would never come. What had made him say such a thing? Michael went into the narrow hall and sat down on the bottom stair, his head in his hands.

He was wet, soaked almost to the skin, and he shivered, and hoped childishly that he would get pneumonia and die. He felt the warm trickle of tears through his fingers, and sobbed with a harsh, dry, racking sound. What a mess, a terrible mess, he had made of things. It wasn't right, it wasn't fair, that a whole life could be wrecked because of a moment of uncontrolled love.

And yet, they could be happy, if only they could live their own lives. Perhaps if he had put the question of the house to Tessa like a proposal? Michael stood up and smoothed his wet hair back with shaking fingers. That was it!

He had never been able to propose to Tessa. Never been able to say: 'Will you marry me?' The marriage had been arranged by her parents with the speed of an urgent military campaign.

Now. Tonight. Tessa would have her proposal. Slamming the front door behind him, Michael began to run.

When he burst into their room, Tessa was sitting on the window seat, staring at the door.

She stood up, and he went straight to her, and held her close. As he began to speak, his voice trembled with the nervousness of a young man proposing marriage to the girl he loves.

'Tessa, sweetheart, I haven't much to offer you. This house is ugly and drab. The paintwork is brown, the ceilings are cracked, and every room will have to be decorated. But we could do it. I know we could.'

He paused, almost gasping for breath. He was tired out, wet, and the unmanly tears pricked at his eyes again. 'Tessa, I'm asking you to come away with me, to start again. Oh, if only you knew how much I love you.'

She didn't speak, and he tilted her chin with his finger and looked deep into her eyes. 'Well, Tessa?' he said softly.

'When you'd gone,' she said, 'I sat and thought. I thought dreadful things; that perhaps you weren't coming back. That you were so angry . . .' she glanced at the books still lying on the floor, 'that you'd never come back. Mummy wanted me to go downstairs to sit with them, and suddenly I realised that all I wanted to do was to sit here quietly, and wait and watch for you. That if you weren't here, then nothing mattered any more.'

Happiness began to float light as a bubble inside him.

'I'll come with you, Michael. Wherever you want to go, I'll come.'

And as he kissed her, he felt in a strange way as if their marriage was just beginning. One in eight marriages doomed from the start, the article had said. But it hadn't taken into account the strength, the resilience of love.

With a suddenly fresh wave of joy he tightened his arms round his young wife.

No More Mountains

When I was asked to be bridesmaid to my cousin Lavinia, I agreed in a half-hearted way. After all, I had been a bridesmaid twice before, and was becoming an old hand at the game.

'There's to be you,' Mother said over the telephone, 'and two tiny ones from the bridegroom's side, Simon and Sally. You remember I told you their mother died when they were only two years old? It was so sad. How that poor man has managed, I don't know. They say he's determined to keep his little family together . . . Are you there, Emma?'

I said that I was.

'It's to be in September, and Lavinia is wearing ivory satin, and they want you to choose an autumn shade, but not gold, because that's the colour Sally's wearing.'

'Isn't Lavinia a bit young to be getting married? She only left school a year ago.'

'She's eighteen and very sophisticated,' Mother said firmly. 'Adrian takes his finals this year. It's a most suitable match.'

Poor Mother. I knew that I was a great disappointment to her. She had started to wear an anxious, harassed look when she talked about my boyfriends, and I had long been aware that to have an only daughter of twenty-five, who was, in her opinion, well on the way to being an old maid, was a definitely shamemaking state of affairs.

Why, I asked myself furiously, as I put the receiver back down and went back to my book, should my single status be a matter of pity, or even ridicule?

It wasn't for the want of being asked, to quote a

common expression. But so far I had met no-one with whom I wished to spend the rest of my life, to love and cherish . . .

I wondered idly who the best man would be at Lavinia's wedding. At my last two weddings it had become quite apparent that they were expected to fall in love with me on the spot.

But this time I needn't have worried. This best man was engaged to a pretty girl with soft, fair hair curling over a black velvet bow worn as a hat, and I saw him turn round and give her a surreptitious wink as we formed our little group on the chancel steps.

Simon and Sally were adorable, dark-haired mites. Sally in golden yellow, with a wreath of flowers on top of her head, and Simon a picture-book page-boy in an ivory satin suit.

I stood behind them, holding Lavinia's bouquet, and thought how sweet they were, and how sad that their mother wasn't here to see how charming they looked.

At that moment Sally turned to her brother, and in a voice which must have carried to the back of the old church, said, 'Softy sissy in that suit.'

Quite deliberately, and before I could move, Simon put out his hand and nipped her hard on the bare flesh of her upper arm, and Sally opened her mouth to howl.

'Stop it! Immediately!' I hissed, and two pairs of eyes, as round and brown as chocolate dragees, surveyed me in astonishment.

'At once!' I said, and sighed with relief as they turned back and stared straight ahead.

Apart from the fact that Sally stood on one leg for most of the time, and Simon chewed an imaginary caramel to try to make her laugh, they behaved themselves for the rest of the ceremony.

At the reception, held in a cleverly converted four-teenth-century barn, a tall man with a thatch of untidy black hair came over to me and shook me warmly by the hand.

'You certainly have a way with children,' he said, his dark eyes crinkling with laughter. 'For a moment, there in church, I thought those two little horrors of mine were going to start a fight. What exactly did happen?'

'You daughter made a derogatory comment about your son in his ivory suit,' I said, and the big man laughed.

'I don't think Simon really knew what he had let himself in for, until the day of the first fitting for his satin suit came along. From then on he's had to be bribed with promises of a visit to the zoo.' Cleverly he intercepted a passing tray, and handed me a glass of sherry. 'I'm sure that bribery would never be advocated in the best of disciplinary circles. Take you, for instance; I'm quiet sure that it's a policy you would never tolerate. Am I right?'

I laughed. 'Does it show so much? That I'm a teacher, I mean?'

He glanced over to the far corner where my mother was talking to the mother of the bride.

'I was, I confess, thoroughly briefed before I came over to you, Emma. You don't mind?'

He held out his hand again, and took mine in a warm clasp. 'Graham Thornton. How d'you do?'

Silently I gave my mother a piece of my mind. What else had she told him, I wondered; and in my embarrassment fell into my usual habit of talking too quickly and too much.

'Bribery would be quite out of place with the pupils in my charge, I'm afraid,' I said. 'No doubt my mother told you that I teach English and History to A-level students at a Technical College. With them it's more a case of subtle persuasion, I'm afraid. Most of my pupils are Lavinia's age. Doesn't she look lovely?'

211

Almost hidden by three tiers of her wedding cake, Lavinia was saying something to her young husband, laughing up at him.

'All brides are beautiful,' said Graham Thornton, and his dark eyes were wistful. I wondered if he was thinking about his own wedding. I felt there was something I ought to say to him, some expression of sympathy; but what was there to say?

Graham nodded towards a chintzy settee.

'The speeches will soon be starting,' he smiled, 'and then you'll have to take your place beside the cake and the bride and groom, and have your virtues extolled by the best man. I speak on the best of authorities, having officiated as best man three times before I married myself.'

'I'm a bit of an expert, myself,' I confided. 'This is my third time as a bridesmaid.'

Then I waited for him to make the obvious rejoinder, that he was sure the phrase, 'Three times a bridesmaid, but never a bride', wouldn't be applicable in my case, but he didn't, and I was glad.

When Sally rushed up to us, flushed and excited with too much attention. and too many fancy cakes, he held her close against his knee, took out the handkerchief again, and wiped her sticky hands.

'Simon's eaten seven cakes, and nine sandwiches, and now he's drinking beer,' she told us in her clear young voice, and we turned round in time to see Simon draining his glass with a flourish that would have seemed quite in keeping if he'd dashed the empty glass against the brass-hung brick fireplace.

Graham stood up. 'Duty calls,' he said, and Sally plucked at his sleeve, and announced that she felt sick – that she was going to be sick – right there.

I started to follow him, but the ceremony of cutting the cake was due to begin, and I had to take my place at the long table.

The best man made a halting, self-conscious speech, thanking me for so ably 'gracing the position', and apologising, amid laughter, for the enforced absence of the other two attendants. The telegrams were read aloud; the cake was cut; Adrian made his speech in which he referred to 'my wife' at least six times, and I whispered to Lavinia that if she wanted to catch their plane, it was time that she went upstairs to change.

As I unzipped her beautiful dress, and she stepped out of it, she turned to me:

'It'll be your turn next, Emma,' she said, 'and oh, I hope that you meet someone like Adrian. He's the most marvellous person. You deserve to find someone like Adrian. I just can't tell you how wonderful he is, and you'll know that he's the one. You will, Emma. Just wait and see.'

There it was again, I thought. That unspoken sympathy with me because of my single state.

There were so many things I had, that Lavinia had given up that very day. My freedom, for instance, my independence, my self-reliance, my flat in town; my chance to travel and see the world; already my application for a year's teaching position in America was in the hands of the powers-that-be. Why should it be assumed that because I was unmarried, I was living what was merely a meaningless existence?

'If you don't hurry,' I said, sounding like the kind of teacher I had vowed I would never become, 'you'll miss your plane. Don't forget you've to be on the receiving end of about a hundred kisses yet.'

'I know,' Lavinia sighed happily. 'And Mummy's sure to cry. . . .'

But Lavinia was wrong. Her mother waved her off quite cheerfully, and, when the car had gone, came over to me.

Graham had chosen the same moment to come up behind me.

'Ah! Emma and Graham!' said Lavinia's mother, coupling our names together as easily as if we'd been engaged for years. 'You'll both be at the party this evening? I do hope so. Weddings are so flat when the happy pair have gone, don't you think?' And she beamed at us fondly.

Graham looked embarrassed, and stroking his chin, murmured something about the difficulty of getting a baby-sitter for a Saturday evening.

I spoke quickly. 'I have to go back to town almost immediately,' I said. 'I'm sorry.'

'Oh, well,' said Lavinia's mother, and walked back across the lawn with the air of having done her best.

There was a subdued twinkle in Graham's dark eyes. 'Sally's feeling much better now,' he grinned. 'She's asleep in the back of the car, and Simon's sulking in the front because he had to miss the wedding cake and the champagne. You don't think I have a potential dipsomaniac on my hands, by any chance?' Then as if he ought to explain himself, he went on: 'I have a housekeeper during the week, but weekends I cope myself, so my Saturday evenings are usually spent watching television or listening to the radio.'

He held out his hand. 'I've enjoyed meeting you, Emma. Perhaps one of these days when I do get up to town, you'll allow me to give you a ring, and we'll have a meal together, and perhaps see a show?'

'That would be nice?' I told him truthfully, lending him my hand for the briefest of minutes, and reflecting wryly that he hadn't even put up the pretence of asking for my telephone number . . .

It was a relief to get back to my flat. I ate a snack supper from a tray, and went to bed with a library book, my third that week.

For the first time ever, it struck me that my careful attention to my own comforts could be interpreted as the beginnings of spinsterish 'little ways'.

I knew, for instance, that I couldn't have got into bed without creaming my face twice; without laying out the clothes I intended to wear the following morning.

I fell asleep with a stupid jingle repeating itself over and over in my brain.

'Emma Smith, Spinster of this Parish,' it said . . .

Usually I enjoyed my Sundays, looking on them as a quiet oasis at the end of a busy, bustling week. A lazy breakfast after a leisurely bath; the Sunday papers, and the gathering up of my laundry for a visit to the launderette the following evening. In the afternoon a film on television, if there were no papers to mark, and out in the evening with the boyfriend of the moment, visiting friends for coffee and conversations.

But this Sunday I was in between boyfriends, and the day seemed to drag on for ever.

I found myself thinking of a big man; a man with unruly dark hair, and an engaging grin, walking across a sun-baked lawn to his car, where, on the back seat, his little daughter lay sick and sorry for herself, and his son sat bolt upright in the front, not a sign of repentance on his round face.

Although Graham was never far from my thoughts during the next week, I was stupidly unprepared for the sound of his voice when he rang.

'I had to do a Maigret act to get your number,' he told me. 'The fact that your surname's Smith didn't help.'

'I did once think of changing it to Smythe,' I told him.

'It wouldn't suit you,' he said promptly. 'And how about Thursday next? I have a meeting in town during

215

the day, and I'd love you to have dinner with me, if you're free.'

I pretended to think for a moment. 'Thursday? Yes, I'm free. That would be lovely. How are the children? Fully recovered?'

'Apart from a couple of rather nasty hangovers on the Sunday, yes, thank goodness.'

I laughed, and we talked of this and that, easily and naturally, and he promised to pick me up about seven.

I tried on my 'little black dress' there and then, decided it wouldn't do, and spent almost a week's salary on a velvet shift in a gorgeous shade of ripe damson.

Graham's dark eyes, when he met me, told me that he liked what he saw, and I noticed with a strange pang of tenderness that he had cut himself slightly while shaving, and that his shirt, of brilliant whiteness, was obviously new.

We talked about the wedding, the twins, the prolonged Indian summer, my job, and our respective tastes in food, music, literature, plays, and television programmes.

When he left me at the door of my flat, I knew that I was already half-way to being in love.

'Will you be coming home this weekend?' he asked me, looking down at me from his great height, and holding my hand far longer than was necessary. 'If you do, and this weather holds, perhaps we can take the twins for a picnic in the woods? Sally's very favourite thing is walking through leaves, and Simon climbs trees like a monkey.'

'I was coming home this weekend,' I lied quite cheerfully, 'and I'm sure the weather will hold. I'll will it to anyway.'

It did, too. That Sunday, the sun glowed in orange splendour from a copper-coloured sky. The air was filled with the scent of wood-smoke, and Sally, in a tiny pair of red wellingtons, scuffed her way through leaf-strewn paths. Simon swinging from branches, called out, 'Watch me, oh please, watch me!'

Graham persuaded me to go back home with them, and I helped to bath the children, and saw them tucked up in their beds.

Then downstairs, in a sitting-room reasonably clean and tidy, but lacking a woman's touch of cushions and flowers, we sat and talked.

Graham put a match to the fire.

'We're due to be clean-air-zoned next year,' he smiled, stretching out his long grasshopper legs to the blaze. 'I'm making the most of the filthy atmosphere while I can. Did you know that there's a leaf caught up in your hair?'

He came over to me then, and I felt the touch of his fingers in my hair. It was one of those moments that any woman recognises. I had only to lift my head, meet his eyes, and I would have been in his arms.

But it was too soon. Graham was older, much older than the boys I had known, and an undefined, instinctive resistance kept me still.

'I'm thinking of taking a teaching post abroad next year,' I said, apropos of absolutely nothing.

Swiftly he moved away, and I heard the springs of his shabby armchair creak as he sat down again.

'Your job means a lot to you, doesn't it, Emma?' he said quietly. 'I do believe you're that rare thing – a dedicated school-marm.' There was laughter in his voice, teasing me, yet with an underlying seriousness. 'And your independence; that means a lot to you, too, doesn't it?' he persisted.

There was far more than normal friendly curiosity in his questions, and I felt confused. A few short weeks ago I could have told him truthfully that my independence meant everything to me, but now I wasn't sure.

'All my life I've been an independent person,' I told him. 'That's why I took my first teaching job away from home. That's why I applied to teach abroad for a year. There's so much I want to see, so much I want to do before I settle down.'

Graham laughed out loud. 'Settling down, as you call it, Emma, is an attitude of mind, not a positive state of affairs.'

Then, with an abrupt change of mood, he was suddenly serious.

'I used to know someone who talked just like you.' For a long moment there was silence between us, and I knew he was thinking about his wife.

'And what happened?' I asked gently.

'She fell in love, and married. It happens all the time,' said Graham.

Simon called down for a drink of water, and after he had finally been pacified, I said that perhaps it was time I went. Graham made no attempt to detain me, but insisted on ringing for a taxi, as he couldn't leave the children alone to take me home himself.

We stood together for a moment at the door as the taxi drew up at the gate.

'Climb all your mountains, Emma Smith,' he said softly, 'and one day come back and tell me all about it.'

It wasn't until I was almost home that the finality of his words struck me forcibly, and I felt unaccountably depressed.

My mother stopped asking me questions when she could see that I was in no mood to answer them.

'That poor man,' she kept on saying. 'He is very much to be pitied.'

And pity, I reminded myself, was said to be akin to love.

After two weeks of waiting for the telephone to ring, dashing to answer it when it did, and then being abrupt to the point of rudeness when the caller turned out to be anyone but Graham, I wrote a letter to the education authorities asking for my application to be expedited.

In December I left my flat and caught a plane to New York, the first stage of my journey to Texas.

The family I stayed with were sweet and kind, and disappointingly English in their outlook. Their daughter Mandy, at thirteen, was completely self-assured, and their small son Gary a precocious bundle of unlimited mischief.

I met Hank during my first term, and he taught me to fish, and to ride, and to eat hamburgers and onions. He was a merry character, and made it clear from the beginning that we would have fun, and not be serious at all. But he had in fact a more serious side to his exuberant nature, and an uncanny perception where I was concerned.

'What is it, honey?' he asked one night. 'Are you homesick or something; or are all English girls like you – not there half the time you're talking to them?'

I apologised and told him truthfully that I wasn't in the least homesick. Not in the way he meant, anyway. Not for green fields and hedges, daffodils in the parks, and walks in the rain . . .

I wrote long descriptive letters to my mother, and she answered each one dutifully, straight away, telling me snippets of gossip, and the news that Lavinia was expecting a baby.

So many times I began a sentence with the words . . . *Do you ever see* . . ., then I would screw the page up and throw it away.

Then one day a letter came with a P.P.S. added at the end. All the more interesting parts of mother's letters were added as non-important after-thoughts . . .

I saw those nice children of that nice man Graham Thornton, she wrote. *They were walking down the high street with their au-pair girl. Swedish I think she is. I heard that the children, especially Simon, are becoming almost unmanageable. They can't get a housekeeper to stay with them.*

An au-pair girl, Swedish. Tall, with straight fair hair, I decided, and blue, blue eyes. Walking along the high street with that indefinable grace; that air of knowing she is beautiful. Sitting opposite Graham in the large and shabby sitting-room, when the children have been put to bed. Smiling at Graham, and talking to him in attractive broken English . . .

The letter fluttered from my hand to the floor.

That summer, the Texan sun shone unmercifully from an azure sky. I remember a day when it rained. Real rain, bouncing up from the dusty roads, and the children ran, laughing, and held out their hands to catch the drops.

'Watch me, Emma. Look at me!' Gary shouted – and there again was Simon swinging from a branch in a sun-dappled wood, calling me in just the same way.

Along with Thanksgiving came the first touch of frost, and Hank took me out for a traditional turkey dinner.

I was to fly back home in time for Christmas, and I told Hank sincerely that I would never forget him, as we exchanged a very sentimental kiss.

'And put that poor guy out of his misery the minute you get back!' said Hank.

Home to the soft, English rain. I bumped into Graham, literally bumped into him, on Christmas Eve. My parcels scattered everywhere.

He was even taller than I remembered, and thinner. The world seemed to dissolve away into nothing as he looked down at me, and I marvelled that time and distance had done nothing to dim my feelings for him.

I asked him about the twins, and he told me that they were in disgrace, having worn out two elderly housekeepers, and two teenage au-pair girls since we last met.

He insisted on running me home in his car, and pointed to the large carton of groceries on the back seat.

'I can whip round the supermarket like a veteran now,' he told me proudly. 'Look what they gave me today.'

From the glove-compartment he produced, with a flourish, a single plastic Christmas rose.

'Welcome home, Emma,' he said softly, and held it out to me.

We were strangely quiet on the short journey home, and outside our gate, when I reached for the door handle, he put his hand over mine.

'Where to now, Emma Smith?' he asked. 'Any more mountains left to climb?'

This time I met his eyes, and what I saw there made my heart thud painfully in my throat.

'No,' I said quietly. 'This time I'm home for good.'

Slowly and deliberately, he drew me to him, and suddenly it was as though all Heaven rocked around me. I clung to him, all the pent-up sadness of the past year fading away as though it had never been.

'The letters I wrote and never posted,' he whispered against my cheek. 'But I had to take the risk. I had to leave you alone to decide for yourself, and I had to be sure, quite sure, that I hadn't seen you right from that very first day simply as a mother for Simon and Sally.'

'And are you sure now?' I said.

'Marry me. Soon,' Graham said, and I turned to kiss him again, and felt the never forgotten touch of his hand on my hair.

As I carried my parcels into the house and through

to my mother in the kitchen, I felt happiness, light as a bubble, almost bursting my heart with joy.

I was thinking how happy she'd be when I told her my news.

For after all, it's not every mother of the bride who gains not only a son on her daughter's wedding day, but two ready-made grandchildren at the same time.

Conversation for One

Here we are, my darling wife, no longer young, but a long way from being old. Twenty-four years married, content with each other, at peace with the world, in spite of the fierce argument we had before we came up to bed.

You are asleep, breathing sweetly, and all around us, the house we have lived in all our married life is quiet and still.

Yes, the peace which needs no understanding is with us, and I glory in it, and hold you close to me . . .

You think you won our argument; you think I am convinced. I have said my piece and will not say it again.

So many of the things you said were right. You are intelligent, you are broadminded and your horizons, unlike those of many of my colleagues' wives, are set far wider than the garden gate. All this I grant you.

I agree that we are no longer living in the Victorian era. I agree that so many of the things we believe in, marriage being but one, are being swept away. We were hypocrites; oh, yes, I'll even grant you that, and if our son, Derek, and his lovely girl friend Sue, see no need to marry, it is no concern of ours.

They are showing their contempt for our old-fashioned notions by openly living together, so we must give them our blessing and wish them well.

What after all is marriage but just a slip of paper? Our son, Derek, was always a good talker and you are convinced. We must move with the times, accept what is now, forgetting what is past.

And I, it seems, am a stick-in-the-mud, a typical product of my over-puritanical background . . .

You murmur something in your sleep, and I suspect that your subconscious mind is still carrying on its argument with me. I stroke your arm, feeling you relax again.

But there are some things you don't know, my darling, some things, please God, that you will never know . . .

If we hadn't been married, if we hadn't gone through all that rigmarole, to quote Derek's phraseology, to obtain that slip of paper, I doubt very much if we would be lying here, warmly content, with our silver wedding anniversary only a few short months away.

Do you remember the year after Derek was born? The way he cried and cried, and the way you devoted yourself to him, almost forgetting my existence?

That was the year I met Gina . . .

She was so pretty, so young and so gay, and she smelt of apple blossom, not of cod-liver oil and baby powder, and you'll never know how much I loved her and how it hurt when we said goodbye for the last time.

I was young then, and thought my heart would break. I think it did break a little, and I was living with you, coming home to you, and because of your obsession with Derek you didn't notice a thing.

How can you love someone, I used to ask myself, and not know when their world has turned itself upside down?

But I was married to you, I was *responsible* for you, and so I sent Gina away.

Then, a long time afterwards, there was Anne. Dark, laughing Anne. She came into my life when your mother came to live with us, and Derek was at school, no longer a baby. That motherly love, which you have

224

in abundance, made you devote yourself to your own mother, as if she were a child.

Oh, she was difficult, I know, and needed you, but *I* needed you, too, and you never guessed how I would sit with you, the two of you, listening to the womanly chatter, feeling an interloper in my own house, watching television with closed eyes, dreaming of Anne.

There was nothing between us, nothing more than a few stolen kisses, a few furtive telephone calls and odd lunches in town. But she made me feel important again. To Anne I wasn't merely a breadwinner, a man who went out of the house at eight o'clock in the morning and came back again at five.

She talked *to* me, not at me. She told me I was clever, and that was heady stuff, but I came to my senses in time. Because I had married you, I had also married your responsibilities; we had promised in the sight of God to love each other till death us did part, and a promise like that isn't lightly tossed aside.

If we had been merely living together, wouldn't I have found it easy to leave you and your mother, apparently quite satisfied with each other? Wouldn't I perhaps, just have taken my things and moved in with Anne?

You'll never know how tempted I was . . .

And you, my love, you must have been all of forty when you met Simon. Oh, yes, I guessed, and by keeping silent, I kept you.

Our marriage by then, had reached the stage when we didn't seem to communicate any more. I had my golf. You had your Women's Guild – forgive me, I know I always get the name wrong – but those were the years when all we seemed to do was to pass at times in the hall and nod, so busy being busy we hadn't time to get to know each other.

Your mother was dead, Derek was away at university, and you were always accusing me of being insensitive. Maybe you were right.

It was no fun being forty-five and working for a firm which was going through the doldrums. No fun seeing other men, younger than I, being handed their redundancy money. I was afraid, very much afraid, and once, when you were wearing a new dress, and had had your hair done a different way, I didn't even notice.

We had a row, a real shouting, husband and wife, glorious clearing-the-air row.

'You take me for granted!' you said. 'You never even *see* me these days,' and, although I wouldn't admit it at the time, I think you were right.

But I did see you. I saw you one day lunching in town with Simon, and I saw the way he looked at you, and I saw what an attractive woman my wife still was, and that day when you came home, your eyes shining and your cheeks flushed, I took you in my arms and said I was sorry for the way I'd been neglecting you.

And you never knew the fear, the blinding fear of losing you, that almost stopped my heart.

Why did you stay with me, my darling? Why did you stop seeing Simon? Wasn't it because we were married?

Wasn't it because divorce is such an ugly thing, a shattering experience, a let's-think-again situation to our generation? Would you have stayed with me, if you could just have walked out?

As Derek and his Sue will feel free to do, with no ties that bind.

Can't you see that?

And if you were awake, instead of sweetly sleeping, and if I could tell you all this, wouldn't you say that it *proves* that we are hypocrites? That the young are right?

So much of what you said downstairs is true. I am no longer sure of what is right and wrong. The so-called permissive society has its repercussions on our age-group too, you know.

But of one thing I am certain, my darling.

That, but for that little slip of paper and all that it signifies, and, more important, all it did signify, I doubt very much if we would be living together like this.

No longer young, but a long way from being old. Twenty-four years married, content with each other, with our silver wedding anniversary only a few short months away. Will Derek and Sue be lying together like this, safe and warm, their testing times behind them, loving each other more than ever because of the times they've stayed, when they could have run away?

I wonder and I doubt, and my heart aches for them.

You sigh in your sleep and murmur something again. tighten my arm around you and you reach for my hand.

It is your left hand, and I feel the ring on your finger and, as I twist it round, your fingers curl round mine.

And now, I can sleep.

The Last Link

The bride was ready, and in ten minutes or so it would be time to leave for the church. There was just one small thing left to do. Louise stared at herself in the mirror, examining herself critically. The navy-blue coat with its cream edging and matching dress underneath had been a good buy. It was a perfect fit, and the hat – a silly froth of cream lace worn straight, showing the minimum of dark hair – flattered her brown eyes.

She leaned forward, worrying for a fleeting second about the careful line she had drawn round her eyes. Was it too much? Too little? Usually she wore only the merest touch of mascara on her long eyelashes; but she had felt that today she could afford to be a little more daring, and her eyes certainly did look bigger – luminous almost. She picked up a coral-tinted lipstick, and then put it down again.

Downstairs her son Jeremy was waiting, no doubt fortifying himself from the sherry decanter and steeling himself for the task of giving his mother away. But really there was nothing to be nervous about. After all, it was only going to be a quiet ceremony, twenty guests, and all of them close relatives or personal friends.

And this evening she would be on a plane with Don, winging across the English Channel to Geneva, where they were to spend the first few days of their honeymoon.

No, there was simply nothing to be nervous about. She loved Don, and he loved her. This was the second time for both of them; and now that their respective children had grown up, they were exchanging the long, lonely years ahead for the serenity and happiness of marriage.

There was just the one small thing left to do . . .

Louise stared down at her left hand, and slowly twisted her wedding ring round and round. The time had come.

'Five minutes, Mother,' Jeremy's voice spiralled upstairs. 'Would you like a sherry?'

'No, thank you, darling. I'll be down in a minute. Have all the others gone?'

'Ages ago,' he shouted back. 'Glynis was in a blind panic. Don't ask me why, and she's forgotten her gloves. Do you think we can take them? She'll die when she finds out.'

Louise smiled. Her young daughter-in-law was always in some kind of panic. Newly-weds!

Louise was watching her reflection in the mirror. By this time she wasn't seeing an elegant woman in her early forties wearing a navy-blue coat and a froth of hat. She was seeing a wartime bride in a white satin dress that had taken most of her precious clothing coupons, with a veil holding back her shoulder-length dark hair.

She was eighteen again, and the man waiting at the church for her was Adrian: tall and slim in his Pilot Officer's uniform, with a forty-eight hours' leave pass in his pocket, and his thick hair touched to fairness in the sunshine which shone through the high stained-glass windows.

'Till death us do part,' they had promised glibly, never dreaming that that would give them only three short years. Death was something that came to other people, even in wartime.

Jeremy had been conceived on their honeymoon, and his memory of his father consisted of the photograph standing on his mother's dressing-table in its silver frame – a photograph of a fair young man with wings on his uniform jacket.

Why had she waited so long before marrying again? Louise turned the ring round and round. Was it because, having known the meaning of true love and losing it so quickly, she hadn't wanted to risk being hurt again?

Once, in his typically unsentimental way, Adrian had said: 'If I should ever buy my ticket, I wouldn't like to think that you were going to spend the rest of your life alone.' But she had stilled his words with kisses, refusing to talk about such a possibility.

Her job as buyer in the evening-gown department of a big store had become all absorbing, and the minute any of her men friends had shown the least sign of becoming amorous, she had sent them away. Even now, after all these years, no one had been able to fill her with the warm delight that being with Adrian had given her. Until Don.

'Mother!' Jeremy's voice was full of urgency. 'The taxi's here.'

Sighing, she pulled at the ring – and found that she couldn't move it past the middle knuckle. She tried again.

She met her own worried expression in the mirror as she pulled and twisted at the thick gold band, but it refused to budge.

Why had she left it until now? Was there some deep psychological reason? Had she perhaps not wanted to remove the last tangible link with her long-lost love?

The eyes in the silver-framed photograph watching her from underneath the peak of the Pilot Officer's cap seemed to be accusing her. Panic was rising thick in her throat.

Her knuckle, already swelling from her frantic efforts, seemed to enlarge with every passing second; and as she ran along the landing, she heard Jeremy's voice filled with agitation, 'Mother, what are you doing? It's time to go.'

Before she closed the bathroom door, she forced herself to answer calmly. 'I'll be down in a minute, darling.'

Heedless of her new coat she ran water into the wash-basin and soaped her finger, working feverishly at the ring.

Only last week, Don had playfully teased her about her refusal to take off her old ring as she tried on the one he had bought for her.

'I'll take it off when the time comes,' she'd told him. 'And that will be just before I leave for the church.'

She remembered how he'd rolled his brown eyes ceilingwards. 'Women!' he'd said. 'I didn't think you went in for that kind of sentimental clap-trap, Louise!'

His tactless words had made her all the more determined. She knew then that she wouldn't remove the ring until the very last minute.

Her heart beating wildly in her throat, she made another despairing effort. The awful possibility of what would happen if she couldn't get it off made her feel sick.

The soap was having no effect, and she ran back into the bedroom, illogical, incoherent reasoning making her jerk open the top drawer of her dressing-table and search madly for a nailfile, scissors – anything.

It was then, as she scrabbled wildly in the drawer, that the eyes in the photograph met her own again. And suddenly, miraculously, her panic left her and she was still. Now the eyes were no longer accusing; they were gazing steadily at her as if trying to tell her something.

Louise leaned against the dressing-table, closing her eyes . . . She was back in church, a nervous bride of eighteen, wearing a white satin dress, and Adrian was trying in vain to force the ring over her finger.

He had got it half-way, and then it stuck. Excitement and nerves had made her hand swell and, as she stood there – the horror on her face mercifully hidden by her veil – Adrian had bent his head towards her, and she had heard his voice, breathing tenderness, 'Relax, darling. Take it easy. Just relax.'

And in the next minute the ring was there on her finger, and the minister was calmly carrying on with the service.

As though he were standing by her side, she heard Adrian's voice again, spanning all those years. 'Relax, darling. Take it easy.'

Holding her breath, she twisted the ring and it slid painfully off her finger. Her heartbeats were steadying now, and limp with relief she heard Jeremy's quick footsteps on the stairs.

And as she placed the ring next to the photograph, she felt the eyes laughing at her, twinkling reassurance as they had all those years ago.

Smiling happily, she followed the broad back of her son down the stairs and out into the sunshine to the waiting taxi.

RC - HOUSE

BINNIE